Faith and Faithfulness

Basic Themes in Christian Ethics

GILBERT MEILAENDER

UNIVERSITY OF NOTRE DAME PRESS

NOTRE DAME   LONDON

Library of Congress Cataloging-in-Publication Data

Meilaender, Gilbert, 1946-
    Faith and faithfulness : basic themes in Chris-
tian ethics / Gilbert Meilaender.
        p.   cm.
    Includes index.
    ISBN 0-268-00982-1
    1. Christian ethics. 2. Faith.   I. Title.
BJ1251.M487 1991   90-50966
241 – dc20   CIP

TO DEREK

Urbem orant; taedet pelagi perferre laborem.

Contents

Preface

In *Three Rival Versions of Moral Enquiry* Alasdair MacIntyre has recently suggested that the history of moral thought and practice suffered a great discontinuity in the post-Enlightenment period, when morality became "a distinct and largely autonomous category of thought and practice," emancipated — as it was hoped — from the web of any background beliefs, especially religious ones. If MacIntyre is correct, moral thinking today will need to be of several different sorts, but perhaps one sort is represented in the chapters that follow, which are an attempt to think about the moral life from within the life of faith.

It is important to note, however, that Christian ethics — as one part of the theological task — must reckon with a still greater discontinuity than that which concerns MacIntyre: that between the old and the new creations. Having completed his little treatise on "The Freedom of a Christian," Luther wrote that it contained the whole of the Christian life in brief form. Because I share in some measure his angle of vision, I characterize the Christian life as one of faith that gives rise to faithfulness. Christians believe that in Jesus God has cared for us. Eternally secure, we are set free to be his agents in caring for others. Put simply, the grace of God frees us to love.

Useful as such a formulation may be, however, it can never capture all that Christian ethics needs to say. We begin in faith; we do not talk only of it. The initial premise—that in Jesus God has cared for us—drives us to ask whether the new life that comes in Jesus is entirely discontinuous from the old life we and others live quite naturally. We may find ourselves wondering whether Jesus alone should be the source of our moral convictions or whether we may rely more broadly upon reasoned moral judgment and reflection. We may wonder whether the new life is simply one of freedom, or whether it is lived within any limits or constraints. Since the new life is not a solo undertaking and is lived within the church, we will be led to reflect upon the role of the church within our world. Since the One in whom we believe now lives beyond the grave, we may be uncertain how we ought to think about and face death. And, perhaps most generally, we may be uncertain how creatures who are deeply rooted in this world are to live with faith in a God who calls us to himself beyond every particular attachment. Such concerns are always pertinent and never trendy—which is to say, worthy of continued attention in theological ethics.

Since we begin in faith, Christian ethics is and ought to be a theological discipline, an attempt to reflect upon the questions to which we are driven by our desire to live faithfully. Christian ethics is therefore singular— developed from within the faith, not from any neutral or universally shared starting point. Nonetheless, that starting point teaches us to think of all human beings in certain ways, to seek and perhaps find common ground with others on some questions, and to value our own naturally and historically given insight. Of course, the very same starting point also teaches us that a life handed over to God must surely entail some transformation of our attachments and projects in life, a transformation so thorough that it will often be experienced as something like a death and resurrection. Faith directs us toward the needs of others. Through our struggle to be faithful, a gracious God transforms

our character and reorients our life — begins to fit us
for communion in God's own life.

From such an angle of vision I approach in the following chapters some of the basic themes in Christian
ethics: our nature as sinful but justified creatures of
God, our place in the natural world, the scope of our
love and the ambiguities of self-love, the relation of
justification and sanctification, the limits on our freedom and our moral knowledge, the relation of church
and world, the meaning of that death toward which we
all journey, the kind of narrative that embodies a life
of faith. No single term — whether faith, love, freedom,
covenant, responsibility, hope, or any of the other great
candidates — captures all that needs to be said on such
topics. Hence, this book cannot be said to contain the
whole of the Christian life in brief form, *except* in the
sense that faith trusts God to pardon our faithlessness
and complete what is fragmentary even in our faithfulness. And, of course, in some moments — in any moment in which we truly encounter the eternal Father
of Jesus Christ — and in every moment, since no moment is divorced from such encounter, no more need
be said. That is the perspective from which faith alone
counts. But the faithfulness to which faith moves us
gives rise to more words — of the sort offered in these
chapters.

How incomplete this book is in relation to what it
aspires to be, I am fully conscious. But it would be
nothing at all were it not for the support I received
from Oberlin College and from the National Endow-
ment for the Humanities — support which gave the time
needed to write. Earlier versions of what have become
chapters one and five appeared in the *Journal of Religious Ethics* and *Faith and Philosophy*, respectively.
I am grateful for permission to use them in revised
form here. Many friends have read bits and pieces of
this manuscript over several years, and I have been
helped by their comments and encouragement. Richard

John Neuhaus read the entire manuscript and reas-
sured me that it was worth saying what I had to say.
In the time since then he has journeyed from Wittenberg to Rome. I trust that these chapters give some
little sense of why one might — and, also, why one might
not.

1. The Singularity
of Christian Ethics

When on my three-foot stool I sit and tell
The war-like feats I have done, his spirits fly out
Into my story: say, "Thus mine enemy fell,
And thus I set my foot on's neck;" even then
The princely blood flows in his cheek, he sweats,
Strains his young nerves, and puts himself in posture
That acts my words.
                                   Shakespeare, *Cymbeline*

Karl Barth, rejecting any "general conception of ethics," turned quite naturally to a metaphor drawn from biblical narrative in order to explain how Christian ethics ought to deal with all such general conceptions of ethics, namely, as "an annexation of the kind that took place on the entry of the children of Israel into Palestine."[1] His view, argued in rich detail, was that "Christian ethics cannot possibly be . . . continuation, development and enrichment" of any such general conception. It is peculiar, distinctive, singular — "the final word of the original chairman."[2] Whether one is attracted or repelled by such forceful claims, the issue Barth raised has continued to be important for theological ethics. And, indeed, the sort of Christian ethic that is not simply a development of some more general conception of ethics has taken on new attractiveness in our time and place — characterized by George Lindbeck as a time when Christianity is "in the awkwardly

1

intermediate stage of having once been culturally established but ... not yet clearly disestablished."[3] One
might argue that in such a time and place any successful transmission of the Christian life must eschew
more general notions of ethics and look to what is sin-
gularly Christian.

This would, to some degree, be a return to what has
been the more normal place of ethical reflection in
Christian theology. For much of their history Christians
did not think of ethics as a discipline separate from
theology. To think about practical consequences of the
faith was simply part of the theological task, carried
out, no doubt, in a rather *ad hoc* manner. Christian
thinkers took up issues as they arose, considering them
within the contours of that larger story they called the
Gospel.[4] Indeed, Augustine's suggestion that Christians
convert to their own use the truths of the philosophers
just as the Israelites had, at God's command, taken the
Egyptian gold, though slightly less aggressively stated
than Barth's view, is much closer to Barth than to any
general or autonomous ethic not grounded in theological
reflection.[5] For such views, 'ethics' specifies that part
of the theological task which tries to discern what 'faithfulness' should mean for those who trust that in Jesus
God has been faithful to his creation.

I. Forms of the Moral Life

What we think ethics is — whether general and gen-
eralizable, or singular and tied to a specific way of life —
will affect our understanding of how the moral life can
best be transmitted. In an essay titled "The Tower of
Babel" and written almost four decades ago, British
political theorist Michael Oakeshott masterfully depicts
the enduring nature of this problem.[6] He outlines two
different forms of the moral life, each an ideal construct
not likely ever to be found in pure form. But if neither

can be lived in undiluted fashion, the crucial question for any society will be which predominates.

For some societies, during at least some part of their history, the moral life may be chiefly what Oakeshott calls "a habit of affection and conduct" (p. 61). That is, moral decisions are not the product of reflective thought, nor are they made by applying a moral ideal or principle to a particular situation. Rather, when this form dominates, we act from habits of behavior — habits taken for granted in the society and inculcated in the young. Ideally, decisions are reached almost without reflection, just as we learn to speak our native tongue without on every occasion of speech pausing to review the rules of grammar and syntax. To read again Oakeshott's description of this form of life is to appreciate how far from it we are today. For this pattern of behavior, he writes, "most of the current situations of life do not appear as occasions calling for judgment, or as problems requiring solutions; there is no weighing up of alternatives or reflection on consequences, no uncertainty, no battle of scruples. There is ... nothing more than the unreflective following of a tradition of conduct in which we have been brought up" (p. 61).

The moral life, conceived in this way, is transmitted in a manner appropriate to its form. Certainly this will not be done chiefly in a classroom, nor by learning — and then learning to apply — a set of moral rules. We might learn a foreign language that way, but "we acquire habits of conduct in the same way as we acquire our native tongue" (p. 62). We learn from those around us — from living with people who habitually behave in certain ways and from being thereby initiated into a tradition of conduct. We have learned to speak English, but there is no moment to which we can point and say, "then I began to learn the language." For it was habitually spoken by all around us. It was the form of life in which we were immersed. To be sure, our language will also have its grammatical and syntactical rules, and the day will probably come when we learn them. Perhaps on one occasion or another they will help us over a difficult point, but this sort of learning has little to do with making us skilled speakers of the language. For education in our native tongue — begun earlier than we could pinpoint — cannot be confined to particular moments. It is the sea in which we float and then, perhaps, swim. "One may set apart an hour in which to learn mathematics and devote another to the Catechism, but it is impossible to engage in any activity whatever without contributing to this kind of moral education, and it is impossible to enjoy this kind of moral education in an hour set aside for its study" (pp. 62f.).

The chief characteristic of this first form of moral life may be the stability it provides both to individuals and their society. This does not mean that moral change never occurs; indeed, it takes place constantly within such a tradition of conduct. Stability comes precisely from the fact that such change is constant, always adjusting to what is new, but never collapsing all at once (in the way a theory can collapse when confronted with a devastating counterexample). We can even recognize the possibility of fairly radical change. A few members of the society may turn out to be gifted poets with a genuine "feel" for the language, and they may speak or write in ways which, though to outward appearances contrary to the rules of the language, in fact extend and enrich it.

If this form of the moral life is not likely to suffer sudden collapse, its chief danger lies in the possibility of gradual degeneration. Precisely because it offers the ability to act without hesitation or doubt, it does not offer the critical ability to analyze and evaluate the shape of the society's moral life. As Oakeshott notes, "from this sort of education can spring the ability never to write a false line of poetry, but it will give us neither the ability to scan nor a knowledge of the names of the various metric forms" (p. 63). As a consequence, lacking any self-critical powers, the society may degenerate into mere superstition (may be unable to distinguish its moral code from a collection of taboos) and may be unable to deal with external challenge based on critical principle.

Oakeshott's second form of the moral life should not be difficult for us to picture, since we come very close to living it. Here "activity is determined, not by a habit of behaviour, but by the reflective application of a moral criterion," whether in the form of ideals or rules (p. 66). From this perspective the moral life requires that we set out its proper form in systematic, connected fashion and then seek to practice it. And it requires of us a kind of critical, self-reflective ability to defend our ideals or rules against all challenges. If, for the first form, conduct tends to be unreflective and free of hesitation, here there must be constant criticism and analysis to determine whether our practice adequately reflects the principles and ideals we have adopted.

In such a society education into the moral life cannot come primarily from observing and practicing appropriate behavior of others. Instead, we will need an intellectual training in the rules or ideals themselves; training in how to apply and defend them. The aim is that each moral agent should act self-consciously, aware of the grounds upon which he acts and prepared to defend those grounds. The image now cannot be that of a language slowly and continuously developing, perhaps even changing considerably when reshaped by one who loves his native tongue and alters it in the spirit of the language itself. Rather, we should think of a language developed for specific purposes — changed in structure and idiom whenever such change will serve business or ideological interests, quantitative precision, or some other concern.

People whose moral life takes this second form are not likely to permit it to become a mere taboo; their life is far too self-critical for that to happen. Its weakness lies elsewhere. It cannot offer the same certainty about how to act that the first form gives. Its adherents will be confident about the criteria for moral decision, but "together with the certainty about how to *think* about moral ideals, must be expected to go a proportionate uncertainty about how to *act*" (p. 68). The constant encouragement of self-reflection undermines the ability to act habitually and confidently. The pause of reflection that is always needed before one acts can paralyze. If the second form of the moral life collapses, it is more likely to happen suddenly than by slow and gradual degeneration. For although its adherents may have acquired considerable ability to resist external, critical challenge, should that resistance be broken, little is left (since their moral life is not undergirded by habit and custom). Mores are likely to change suddenly and rapidly.

The moral life of any living community is likely to combine these two forms. And as Oakeshott himself notes, this is for the best. "Neither, taken alone, recommends itself convincingly as a likely form of the moral life, in an individual or in a society; the one is all habit, the other all reflection" (p. 70). Put more theologically we could say: The one thinks of the human person solely as a finite being, located in a particular time and place, without any ability to transcend that location. The other imagines that the person is all freedom, limited in no way by the constraints of finitude.

Even if neither of these forms of the moral life, taken by itself, can be recommended, there have of late been powerful voices — both theological and philosophical — suggesting that we need to recapture something closer to Oakeshott's first form: moral life as habitual behavior learned in the way we learn our native tongue. Indeed, this is a theme which may prove to have considerable appeal as we near the end of the second millenium of the Christian era and begin to contemplate the shape of Christian existence in the twenty-first century.

The philosopher Alasdair MacIntyre has suggested that our historical location can be compared to the time (in the fourth to sixth centuries) when the Roman Empire, its energies dissipated and unable to find any effective principle of political cohesion, declined into the Dark Ages.[7] In such circumstances, MacIntyre argues, we must do what some did then: direct our attention to constructing and maintaining new forms of community in which the moral life can be sustained, however dark the age may be which comes upon us. Indeed, for MacIntyre we are not caught in some awkwardly intermediate stage. The barbarians are already in control! Ours is a world in which the moral life has no agreed-upon basis or structure. We imagine that we must find moral standards which can meet with universal acceptance even while we tend (in our subjectivist hearts) to believe that moral arguments can never be settled. We call loudly for a more meaningful public life to sustain our individual pursuits, but what we really care about—and will sacrifice for—are private goals and purposes. Ours is, in short, a badly fragmented society. In these circumstances, MacIntyre cryptically suggests, we await a new St. Benedict, who can teach us how to fashion communities in which the moral life can be sustained.

MacIntyre's analysis and prescription are akin to George Lindbeck's hope for a small minority of Christians clearly delineated from their "dechristianized" surroundings and authentically devoted to the cultivation of their own way of life. Lindbeck is, if anything, less hopeful than MacIntyre. When he looks at church and society he finds for the most part a "disarray" which makes it increasingly difficult to transmit and inculcate a way of life. He first attributes such disarray only to certain elites, "those who share in the intellectual high culture of our day."[8] But a few pages later it turns out that the forces of modernity have so "dissolved the bonds of tradition and community" in our world that "multitudes" can think of the religious life only in terms of an individual, idiosyncratic quest. Worst of all, rather than being "communities that socialize their members into coherent and comprehensive religious outlooks and forms of life," the churches have pandered to this trend.[9] Hence, our situation is desperate: We can no longer depend on a society at least roughly Christian to socialize its members into anything approaching a Christian way of living, nor can we recapture the kind of serious catechesis by means of which the church once inculcated its way of life even amidst an alien culture.

I am not myself persuaded that ours is as fully post-Christian a culture as these diagnoses suggest, however compelling and even commonsensical such descriptions may seem to those who—whether by choice or fate—spend their lives in academic institutions. There are all around us at least partial bits of evidence for a resurgent ability of Christians to shape the moral life of our society.[10] If these attempts are often unpopular, that should hardly surprise those whose own diagnoses suggest a culture in considerable tension with Christian vision. And we must remember that even the *corpus christianum* was considerably less monolithic than our myths imagine. For example, in a book exploring what he called "the foundations of Western cultural singularity" in medieval experience, the historian Francis Oakley pointed to pluralism in the economic realm. During the medieval period the church ultimately failed in its effort to impose an economic ethos shaped by the constraints of church teaching (with respect to usury, just wages, and prices). In fact, Oakley writes, "already by the eleventh and twelfth centuries, Europe had become politically too pluralistic, too fragmented, too disorderly, either to sponsor or to admit the successful imposition upon all groups of a single standard of economic behavior."[11] Pluralism already! — long before the rise of MacIntyre's barbarians or Lindbeck's dechristianized world.

Having said this, I would not wish to deny a good measure of truth to the diagnosis of our cultural predicament offered by MacIntyre and Lindbeck. To the degree that it is true, what kind of prescription for the moral life of the church should follow? Should the emphasis in Christian ethics fall on generality, on the attempt to find common ground with all ways of life? Or on singularity, on the attempt to think through the peculiar shape of the Christian life? The choice we are given is stark: either renewed attention by the church to its own way of life, or dissipation into and absorption by the larger society, which likes nothing better than a cultural Christianity. An analogy Lindbeck uses may remind us of Oakeshott. Learning to live as a Christian is not like learning a set of principles and how to apply them; it is more like acquiring the skills needed to use a language. Indeed, calling irresistibly to mind Barth's claim that the Christian life deals with other, general conceptions of ethics as the Children of Israel annexed the promised land, Lindbeck suggests that Christians must live in such a way that "it is the text ... which absorbs the world, rather than the world the text."[12] Here, indeed, is an emphasis upon singularity. We may even, with due caution, term such a prescription 'sectarian'.[13] At the conceptual level it will not tend to assume that there is or should be any continuity between the ethic which shapes the life of communities of believers and the morality of the surrounding non-Christian society. At a more institutional level the prescription will emphasize the need for renewed attention to ways in which the church inculcates and transmits its own peculiar vision of life.

In the chapters which follow I will myself give considerable attention to the particular shape of the Christian life — to the commitments of believers and to the way in which those commitments form moral vision. All the more important, therefore, to recognize at the outset that neither of Oakeshott's forms of the moral life, taken alone, can be recommended. All the more reason to work through the limitations of an emphasis on the singularity of Christian ethics. To think of the Christian life as a moral tradition learned in the way we learn our native language is useful; it directs our attention to the truth that ethical reflection and moral theory cannot generate or sustain that way of life. But a way of life which involved only that kind of learning would be deficient—precisely from a Christian perspective. In particular, it would fail to make place for freedom—freedom of the human person, and the freedom of God.

II. Human Freedom

Human freedom is endangered—and human nature misunderstood—if we make no place for the person's ability to transcend his biological and historical location, for our ability to find common moral ground with those whose location is very different. And to think of the Christian life as analogous to a language may, unless sharply qualified, entice us into too easy a relativism in theology and ethics. The analogy, essentially a historicist one, encourages us to think of the "oughts" and "ought nots" of a moral tradition as we think of linguistic prohibitions. One ought to be faithful to one's spouse—as one ought to have a subject and predicate in a sentence. We must not permit retarded newborns to go without lifesaving medical care—as we must not split an infinitive or end a sentence with a preposition. And noting that many or most such linguistic rules are required only in certain languages, we may come to regard them as arbitrary. Would we, after all, worry about split infinitives if English had not been shaped in important ways by the Latin language? This does not make the rules of English grammar and syntax any less binding on speakers of the language, but it embeds those rules in a particular history which will not be shared by speakers of other languages. There could be other ways to live—as there could be other ways to communicate. This happens to be ours. It serves our needs well. Indeed, we enjoy its distinctiveness and its peculiarities, though, of course, we recognize that others might choose to live (or speak) differently and that their choices could be as reasonable as ours.[14] Among such different forms of life there may be no compelling grounds for rational choice. Armenian is not a better or worse language than English, only a different one. This is where the language analogy tends to lead—to different forms of life, one of which just happens to be ours.[15]

There are, of course, aspects of any way of life—including the Christian life—which are important primarily because they have come to be deeply embedded in a pattern of conduct which we esteem and desire to continue. Burial customs are a common illustration. And in their discussions of monogamy and polygamy Christians have sometimes been uncertain about the degree to which their appreciation for and advocacy of monogamy is like the linguistic rule telling us not to split an infinitive. But we need only think of the Decalog, as Christians have tended to read it, in order to realize that some elements of the Christian way of life are probably essential aspects of almost any shared, common life. Few societies can survive which do not pay careful attention to the bonds toward which the second table of the law points: the bond of parents and children, of spouses, of life with life, of persons and property, and the bond by which speech is a manifestation of the self.[16] No doubt the richness and texture of a way of life cannot be understood fully or transmitted succesfully through appeal only to such common moral concerns, even as it may be true that no language can be translated without loss. But there is at least some common moral ground available to people in quite different social circumstances, just as translation of languages *is* possible, and this common ground cannot simply be absorbed by Christian vision. It retains a certain independence. For there is more to being human than can be accounted for by our immersion in any way of life, and our experience is not fully circumscribed by the language we speak. Those who regularly recite the first article of the creed, desiring their world to be shaped by that recital, should expect this. They should anticipate that human beings share a common bond which will enable them to meet — to "translate" to some extent their ways of life and understand each other. Thus Augustine read the story of creation: "God created man as one individual; but that did not mean that he was to remain alone, bereft of human society. God's intention was that in this way the unity of human society and the bonds of human sympathy be more emphatically brought home to man, if men were bound together not merely by likeness in nature but also by the feeling of kinship."[17]

Since, by virtue of God's creation, human beings share a common nature, they are not limited entirely by their particular social and historical locations. They are free to seek common moral ground with confidence that at least some may be found. Hence, our shared nature provides a partial corrective to historicist tendencies. But our freedom from any particular location is not grounded solely in a shared human nature. That humanity is the creation of God, and our freedom is, finally, a freedom for God. The same creed which teaches us to anticipate a common nature also depicts the human being as a creature made for God — whose heart is restless apart from God and who must therefore transcend even the most universal of historical communities. Hence, our freedom makes theories of a universal morality grounded in human nature or reason possible but also problematic: *possible* because it is the human capacity for free transcendence that enables us to find common, even potentially universal, moral ground; *problematic* because, since we are ultimately free for God, the generality required for a universal morality will always stand in some tension with the freedom of God. Our capacity to *transcend* all historical communities implies the possibility of *transforming* them. Our task, therefore, is always a complicated one: to affirm and live in the world God has created while constantly transforming our given communities on the way to the promised rest in God.

Josef Pieper once described the distinctive mark of the Christian West as "theologically grounded worldliness."[18] *Worldliness* — that is, an appreciation of natural reality and a recognition that its existence cannot simply be absorbed by Christian vision. *Theologically grounded* — because all worldly realities are created by God and can become "instruments and vehicles of salvation in the sacramental process." This means that all realms of natural life — science, technology, political power, labor and work, erotic love — have a created existence of their own and can be investigated and understood, at least partially, in their own terms. At the same time, if this worldliness is theologically grounded, no aspect of created reality can be fully understood apart from the Creator, and when taken into the Christian life the natural realm must "submit to a transformation and reshaping" in accord with the norms of Christian knowledge. Such theologically grounded worldliness has been the basis for a "world-affirming and world-forming theology," but not, let us note, for a world-absorbing theology.

The tension between these two elements — worldliness and theological ground — gives rise to both instability and dynamism in the Christian life; for our effort must be not simply to think them together but "to *live* them together." No code for carrying out such a task can be given; it must be a free human venture. Pieper himself characterizes the combination as "explosive" and "dangerous," and he writes that the fusion of these two elements "cannot be achieved once and for all. It is not to be expected that a final balance can ever be reached." When within the lives of Christians the natural world is reshaped, it is both affirmed and (sometimes drastically) transformed. This means instability — since no social structure can be perfected or can offer an abiding city. And it means dynamism — since, short of the coming kingdom, even stable Christian communities can be only "on the way." We should not ask for more than this as a Christian way of life.

One of the best examples of this tension is the attempt in our civilization to join romantic love and the faithfulness of *agape* in the institution of Christian marriage. In this union the power of *eros* is taken seriously. If it is reshaped when brought within Christian marriage, it is not absorbed, and it is even correct to say that within our society the worldly passion of romantic love penetrated the Christian understanding of marriage and suffused it with "a greater tenderness and mutual esteem."[19] *Eros* was affirmed. Christians learned from it while at the same time they sought to transform it. If romantic love, fickle as it is, promises faithfulness, Christians were bold enough to claim that *eros* could be fulfilled — could be what it claimed to be — only when brought within the transforming power of *agape*. To be sure, such a combination must always be unstable; either love can threaten to absorb or extinguish the other. On the one hand, if *eros* does not submit to transformation and correction, we will conclude that, since falling in love was a good reason to marry, falling out of love (or into love with someone else) must be a good reason to break the marital bond. But on the other hand, if the call for fidelity extinguishes our appreciation for the power and beauty of erotic love, we will not see how great a sacrifice we sometimes ask — albeit rightly — when we grant *agape* governance in our understanding of marriage. What we speak of as — and believe to be — fulfillment may be experienced as something closer to destruction.

What Pieper wrote of civilization in general is, then, true of the institution of marriage in particular. The fusion of romantic love and Christian faithfulness in marriage "cannot be achieved once and for all. It is not to be expected that a final balance can ever be reached." *Eros* is continually transformed by *agape* even while the attempt to be faithful to the needs of one's spouse is constantly instructed by the passion and power of romantic love. This is the way the Christian life is, in fact, lived as theologically grounded worldliness. We would be somewhat misled if we took too seriously Lindbeck's metaphor of "absorption." The world should not be absorbed by Christians — whether in a sectarian or a Eusebian manner. It must be affirmed *and* transformed by those who know that the tension between affirmation and transformation cannot be overcome in this pilgrim existence.

III. The Freedom of God

We may say, then, that by giving too little place to human freedom, the first form of the moral life — moral life as akin to a native language — misses the common human bonds toward which the Christian understanding of creation points and too easily encourages us to miss the dialectic of affirmation *and* transformation which should characterize our relation to the world. We turn now to another difficulty, one grounded more in God's freedom than in ours, more in the second and third than the first article of the creed. Once again Josef Pieper can point the way. Discussing the possibility of transmitting the faith, he put his finger square-

ly on the crucial issue. "In no epoch, no matter how
'Christian' it may have been, have faith and hope been
so readily available to man that he has had only to
reach out for them. That is an inexorable fact; it may
be forgotten, but it cannot be altered, however much
we are on a familiar footing with the divine Mystery
in our speech and thought."[20]

To the degree that Christian life conforms to Oakeshott's first model, the behavior which love requires
and trust and hope empower becomes habitual—a possession ready at hand. The community appears to sustain itself as it passes on a stable pattern of affection
and conduct. Moral vision and right activity are skills
cultivated by the community, inculcated in the young,
and possessed by the mature. Theologically, the model
seems to call for a period of intense and lengthy cate-
chetical instruction followed, eventually, by baptism of
those who have become proficient and skilled in the
Christian life. This is suggested by Lindbeck's description of the early church, a description which in context
seems also to imply a recommendation:

> Pagan converts . . . submitted themselves to prolonged
> catechetical instruction in which they practiced new modes
> of behavior and learned the stories of Israel and their
> fulfillment in Christ. Only after they had acquired profi-
> ciency in the alien Christian language and form of life
> were they deemed able intelligently and responsibly to be
> baptized.[21]

Can this be an adequate understanding of the Christian life—its possibilities, and the means for sustaining
it? Certainly there is much truth here. This model recognizes that Christian character—our vision and our
action—cannot be sustained apart from communities
which seek diligently to shape that character and make
it habitual. "Where your treasure is, there will be your
heart also," Jesus says.[22] The heart—the character of
the person—will be formed by action and conduct. But

this movement from conduct to character does not capture all that must be said about Christian virtue; for there is also the movement from character to conduct, from the heart to the action it makes possible. "Either make the tree good, and its fruit good; or make the tree bad, and its fruit bad; for the tree is known by its fruit. . . . For out of the abundance of the heart the mouth speaks. The good man out of his treasure brings forth good, and the evil man out of his evil treasure brings forth evil."[23] Put most simply: the Christian community does not sustain itself or its way of life. That life does not become its possession; for it is sustained by the free grace of God. The community does not play the decisive role in shaping the life of its children—a truth which receives eloquent witness when it hands those children as infants over to God in baptism with the prayer that their hearts may be created anew and that from such a heart the virtues of faith, hope, and love may flow.

The comparison between learning to be a Christian and learning one's native tongue is in many ways instructive. But its tendency is to make this way of life our possession, to underplay our radical dependence on God's free grace, to seduce us into thinking that we are on so familiar a footing with the divine mystery that we need only reach out for a readily available faith and hope.

Perhaps it may be instructive to change the analogy—from learning to speak to learning to write. In 1959 E. B. White published his revised edition of *Elements of Style* by William Strunk, Jr.[24] The resulting hybrid—Strunk & White—must be one of the very few enjoyable texts ever written about syntax and grammar. In his revision White added a chapter titled "An Approach to Style," which is in many ways not just about writing but about morality. White suggests that good writing shapes character; for it calls for certain habits of behavior, a kind of attentiveness and self-discipline. "The act of composition, or creation, disciplines the mind; writing is one way to go about thinking, and the practice and habit of writing not only drain the mind but supply it too" (p. 70). That is to say, attention to one's treasure forms one's heart.

If, however, this were all good writing required, we could by dint of effort and attention fill our schools with good writers. If no more needed to be said, good writing could be taught—even as the Christian way of life could be passed on readily enough if it were only habits of behavior sustained and transmitted by a community skilled in such conduct. But more *is* neeeded to explain skilled writing. "Who can confidently say what ignites a certain combination of words, causing them to explode in the mind?" White asks (p. 66). Consider, he suggests, the sentence, "These are the times that try men's souls." It would be possible to rewrite this sentence in other, grammatically acceptable ways. White offers four possible rewrites:

> Times like these try men's souls.
> How trying it is to live in these times!
> These are trying times for men's souls.
> Soulwise, there are trying times.

What makes Thomas Paine's sentence memorable and the alternatives eminently forgettable? To answer that question would be to make some progress toward answering another: What makes the Christian life more than a community possession that is readily available for handing on?

Good writing has a certain style which cannot be learned or acquired simply from attention to the mechanics of language. Yet, even while affirming that, White continues also to affirm that learning to write well may help to impart a characteristic style to our writing. Attention to writing develops style—but good writing has a style which cannot be taught. If we become perplexed at this seeming paradox, we are ready to consider White's conclusion to his essay. He points to the secret while commenting on two lines in a poem by Robert Louis Stevenson—lines which he regards as particularly excellent. Stevenson wrote of a cow "blown by all the winds that pass / And wet with all the showers." And suddenly, White says, "one cow, out of so many, received the gift of immortality. Like the steadfast writer, she is at home in the wind and the rain; and, thanks to one moment of felicity, she will live on and on" (p. 85). This is the secret White discerns: the gulf between good mechanics and true style is bridged only in a "moment of felicity." He appeals to the Muse. And it is noteworthy that, in commenting on White's approach to style, his biographer is driven to the language of religion. "White's parting explanation, that good writing occurs in moments of felicity, does not undercut his instruction in the art of writing well. It only reminds the reader that though an approach to style can be taught, the achievement of memorable writing is a miracle. To be sincere he had to say so."[25]

And to be likewise sincere, Christians must say the same about their way of life. It is not a possession sustained through their own efforts to cultivate it. And however attentive they may be and ought to be to the shape of their corporate life, the image of the baptized infant handed over to God for safekeeping and new creation will suggest their continuing dependence upon the free grace of God and the centrality in the Christian life, not of moral effort and discipline, but of trust.

IV. The Singularity of Christian Ethics

We have, then, found reasons to draw back from too sectarian a prescription for Christian ethics. The image of Christian life as insider's knowledge, as a moral tradition learned in the way we learn our native tongue, cannot be fully adequate. Even if Christian moral

knowledge is built upon no foundation other than the
biblical narrative of God's dealings with his world, that
story itself authorizes us to seek and expect some common moral ground with those whose vision is not
shaped by Christian belief. Thus, although the Christian way of life is itself a particular one sustained within particular communities, it has within it more
universal elements. And the understanding of life
which faith seeks, if it is truly understanding, will to
some extent admit of "translation" into the language
of public life — which life it both affirms and seeks to
transform. Moreover, biblical faith calls for trust in the
free God, whose grace alone can ultimately sustain the
life of discipleship in the world. For all these reasons
it seems best to describe Christian ethics as a two-tier
ethic — in part general and able to be defended on
grounds not peculiarly Christian; in part singular, making sense only within the shared life of the faithful
community. Having recognized the generality, we return now to the singularity that is suggested by the
analyses of MacIntyre and Lindbeck.

To try to explain the Christian life to those who know
little of the biblical story and do not practice its disciplines will be difficult. In such explanation we limit
ourselves to the barest essentials of belief, to those
elements (torn from a larger fabric) which seem to hold
universal appeal. At best we are likely to leave unsaid
much that is important; at worst we may offer for public
consideration a collection of abstracted fragments
which can look like little more than an unwarranted
selection of moral eccentricities. It is simply the case
that Christian moral vision is not fully available apart
from the virtues authorized by biblical narrative and
formed by the disciplines of Christian life.

Only some understanding of their way of life will
explain why Christians — unwilling to love father or
mother more than Jesus — might make a decision for
celibacy and the monastic life. Or why they might have

grave reservations about any genital relationship which was, throughout its history, nonprocreative not by accident but by intent. Or why they would think marital faithfulness called for even in a marriage which promised little growth or fulfillment. Or why they might refuse to relieve the suffering of a dying man by aiming at his death or starve a newborn who was destined to be retarded. Or why they would not make survival the chief goal of public policy. Christian talk of obedience to parents, is, finally, not separable from talk of the family of the church, a bond open to all. Christians measure faithfulness in marriage by the standard of Christ's commitment to his bride, the church. Whatever they may think it necessary to render to Caesar and however much they may recognize the necessity of government's sword, they bend the knee to a God crucified by the political powers of his day. Every week they rededicate the tongue to the praise of God, and they offer back their possessions to the One who gave them. No doubt it would be possible to teach the basic principles of the Decalog apart from this background of belief, but such general reflection would not sustain the possibility of the Christian life. It would be more like studying Esperanto than like learning English as one's native language. Perhaps such views cannot be transmitted or fully comprehended apart from the opportunities for confession, praise of God, and instruction in the biblical story which Christian community ought to provide. Only as our character is shaped in these ways will we be able to see what trust in God calls for and makes possible.

For a more extended illustration of the point we can consider a topic much debated in recent years: abortion. Stanley Hauerwas has argued that most recent Christian attempts to explain "why abortion is an affront to our most basic convictions about what makes life meaningful and worthwhile" are doomed to failure; for these accounts, attempting to make only those appeals thought permissible in the public realm, abstract Christian conviction from the stories which shape Christian life.[26] Here again, we could easily overstate the point. That the Christian way of life — and, indeed, its power and attraction — cannot be made fully intelligible within the restrictions of the public sphere does not mean that no common ground or possibilities for "translation" exist. So, for example, the political theorist Philip Abbott suggests that we consider as a possible general law of social science the claim: "the restriction of the concept of humanity in any sphere never enhances a respect for human life. It did not enhance the rights of slaves, prisoners of war, criminals, traitors, women, children, Jews, blacks, heretics, workers, capitalists, Slavs, Gypsies. The restriction of the concept of personhood in regard to the fetus will not do so either."[27] Perhaps there is common meeting ground to be found between Abbott's proposal and Christian vision; for however often that vision may have been used to restrict the boundaries of humanity, it has also helped shape a history in which such limits have been subjected to criticism and, time after time, shattered.

But the possibility of such common ground is not the same as an elaboration of the Christian vision of life, and it leaves unsaid much that Christians may sometimes wish to say. Perhaps the simplest and most striking way to put this Christian vision is to say: We are — all of us — fellow fetuses.[28] All without the ability to speak for themselves in the court that really counts — before God — and in need of a vindicator to speak on our behalf. All without claims or achievements that count for anything in that divine court and in need of a defender who will uphold the rights of the poor and needy. All compelled to trust One more powerful than we.

Indeed, if the Bible has any central theme, it may be that God acts to save those who cannot save themselves. That in carrying out this saving activity he is no respecter of persons—but values the strong and the weak, the rich and the poor, the female and the male, the black and the white, the born and the unborn. We are called to love in like manner. Israel, knowing itself to have been chosen of God though nothing among the nations, is commanded then to care for the stranger in the land. Christians, knowing that God has chosen what is weak in the world to shame the strong, are commanded to love as Christ has loved us. Such love will be radically ill at ease in a world where worth is measured in terms of achievement, or mental capacity, or power, or whether someone else wants us. To know ourselves as fellow fetuses must mean that we will be very reluctant indeed to narrow the bounds of the human community.

G. K. Chesterton once pointed out that we should not underestimate the importance and power of the Christmas story to shape the lives of believers. Those pictures we have seen since we were young children, those stories we have heard told time and again—all, as Chesterton put it, ringing the changes on a single mysterious theme: that the hands that made the sun and stars were once too small to reach the huge heads of cattle in a stable.[29] We welcome children into our midst, therefore, not because we can protect them from all the dangers of life, not because they are lovable little things, not because their potential is great—but as a renewed act of trust in the God who has taken upon himself the dangers and problems of our life. Something like this—and no doubt much more—would have to be said if we were to get to the root of Christian opposition to most abortion.

In any case, understanding the simple prohibitions of the Decalog is an ongoing task of the Christian community, a conversation which never ends. For the aim is not simply to understand a few rules but to set forth a way of life. After all, Luther's *Small Catechism* grew out of his experience visiting the parishes of Saxony.

It was intended to be taught—but taught within the ongoing life of a worshiping community of believers. Abstracted from that way of life, particular rules for Christian living may lack intelligibility and will almost surely lack the power to persuade or the beauty to attract. If the way of life could be formulated in relatively brief compass, there would be little need for the church's worship to be framed within a liturgical year which takes the Christian's life into the story of God and his covenant people, a story which—as that liturgical year itself makes clear—must continue until the end of human history. Ethical reflection alone, however critical or perceptive, cannot itself supply this rich background for moral deliberation and decision. If the preaching, teaching, and worship of the church do not help Christians see their world within the framework provided by the biblical story, no narrative theology or narrative ethics can supply what is lacking. That there should in recent years have been so much interest in theology and ethics which are narrative in character, that there should have been attempts to analyze liturgies and show their significance for the moral life— all this serves chiefly to indicate our continued need for and felt lack of Oakeshott's first form of the moral life: a tradition of behavior lived habitually and unreflectively. This can be given only when in worship we "hear a bit of the Word at a time."[30]

V. Generality within Singularity

The interplay of generality and singularity—as important for the entire theological enterprise as for theological ethics—has perennial significance. But it was made central in this century by Barth, and its continued centrality forces upon us certain questions: Is theology concerned primarily to explore the way in which religious belief answers certain fundamental questions of human experience? Or, is its chief concern exploration of the grammar of a particular religious way of life? It may prove fruitful to approach this question briefly in terms of Helmut Thielicke's distinction between "Cartesian" and "non-Cartesian" forms of theology.[31]

Cartesian theology focuses on the believability of Christian kergyma. Intent on asking about the significance of the message and about how one can come to believe it, theologians of this stripe make central the self-understanding of the person who hears the message. It must make sense to us, must speak to our concerns. In order to help this happen, Cartesian theologians try to fit the message into our life and self-understanding, try to make place of it within our vision of reality. The danger, of course, is that human self-understanding becomes the filter through which the word of God must be strained and the criterion which determines what God may say — even though, because we are sinful, our self-understanding is "a perverted and mythicized reality rather than the true one" (p. 144).

By suggesting that we can fit God into the world we (sinners) have created, Cartesian theology misses to some extent the way in which God challenges, transforms, and, even, destroys the perverted realities we construct. In worlds of our making, Thielicke writes, "God can live only on the cross" (p. 146). The notion that we can detect in universal human experience some "point of contact," a "vestibule" of human self-understanding through which God's word can enter, forgets that our own self-understanding must also be crucified in order that there may be "a resurrection beyond this world and against it" (p. 146). The work of the Spirit "does not just ring a bell in an existing pre-understanding but it creates its own hearers" (p. 60). Hence, one might argue that the theological task is simply to report the new self-understanding that has been given through the Holy Spirit and to explore the way of life to which that Spirit's activity gives rise.

The issue, as Thielicke frames it, seems a straightforward one: "Do I draw the creative Word into my self-consciousness so that it is integrated into this and can no longer be regarded as a creative Word but only as one that modifies this self-consciousness? Or does the creative Word draw me into its sphere of influence, so that I am integrated into the salvation event which works on me, and to that extent am referred to something outside myself?" (pp. 193f.). Having posed the issue this way, however, Thielicke proceeds to complicate it. There is also something to be said *for* the concerns of Cartesian theology, even if those concerns should not be allowed to dominate the theological task. The kerygma is an address, and it calls for free human response in love rather than slavish obedience. It is, of necessity, always spoken into some "vestibule," a place where some self-understanding and some questioning already exist. If this were not seen and affirmed, our humanity—which is, of course, God's creation—would be entirely disregarded.

> If man is a vacuum and the Holy Spirit is the substance that fills it, we had better speak of physics rather than theology. A personal relation between God and man is impossible on this level. If this level is to be avoided, if the Word of God, the kerygma, is to encounter a concrete man with a specific self-understanding, then theological relevance must be ascribed to what is already there for the kerygma. . . . Without this appropriation the kerygma remains outside or else it forces its way in as law, and is no true gospel. (p. 138)

This problem—the possibility of continuity between our created humanity and the revealed grace by which God re-creates—is a permanent one within Christian theology. And in some way both continuity and discontinuity must be affirmed. We can see this, for example, in the central event of the gospel, the resurrection of

Jesus. On the one hand, the risen Lord displays the marks of the nails in his hands to demonstrate that he is Jesus who was crucified. On the other, the risen Lord is more than a resuscitated corpse; his life is that of the world to come, and his continuity with Jesus of Nazareth can never simply be demonstrated. To require that the Christian message accommodate itself to human understanding allows no place for such death and resurrection of the self. But to ignore the self who is addressed by the message would make the gospel simply news from elsewhere rather than good news that speaks to the need of sinful creatures. The language of continuity — that God intends to perfect rather than destroy our created nature — can be believed, and we may trust that retrospective vision will one day see its truth. But the language of discontinuity — that death and resurrection of our self-understanding is necessary — must often be the experience of Christians.

Theology cannot therefore proclaim itself "non-Cartesian" and ignore the "vestibule" of self-understanding, the context into which the message is spoken and of which it must make sense (even while overturning and transforming it). Put in Johannine terms, we may say that when the Word becomes flesh, he comes not to what is alien but to "his own." But if the dangers of Cartesian theology are to be avoided, it is important that this vestibule itself be understood in ways that are governed by the story of salvation unfolded in the Bible. Thielicke notes two different ways in which biblical narrative develops a context into which the gospel may be spoken.

One way, most immediately compelling for communities already shaped by the story of Israel in the Old Testament, is to read that story as a history of promise — the fulfillment of which comes, then, in the story of Jesus. Another way — perhaps of more universal appeal, yet still not a way based solely on philosophical analysis of the possibilities for human understanding—is to speak of Jesus against the background of "the sketch of human existence in Genesis 1-11—man's created, fallen, and yet preserved existence" (p. 64). This second way, since it offers more general possibilities for speaking of human nature, can capture some of the concerns of Cartesian theology. It can lend itself to general discussion of human experience without wrenching human beings out of relation to God. Perhaps it was something like this that Barth had in mind when, in the midst of a slashing attack on any nontheological ethic, he permitted himself (in, to be sure, a small print excursus) to find in certain novelists an acceptable "nontheological" ethic "that knew the limits of humanity, and would not therefore treat humanity as an absolute, but would for that very reason do justice to it and serve it."[32] To make such a concession, to construct this sort of vestibule, is to begin to make room for the more universal appeals necessary for Oakeshott's second form of the moral life.

We can illustrate these two approaches and, in fact, see them operating in close proximity if we consider a few key words in St. Paul's Letter to the Galatians: gospel (*euaggelion*), promise (*epaggelia*), law (*nomos*), and faith (*pistis*). If we attend to Paul's use of these words in Galatians, we discover two quite different ways of picturing the encounter between a believing human being and God—ways that correspond to the two sorts of pre-understandings described by Thielicke. The distinction is, roughly, between Paul's language in 2:14-3:12 and his language in 3:13-41. The figure of Abraham ties the sections together; yet, Abraham's faith is spoken of in quite different ways.

At first, *faith* is primarily subjective trust on the part of an individual. There is no indication that the time of faith and the time of law are antithetical, but, instead, faith is set in contrast to *works of law* (the locution most common in 2:14-3:12). The question Paul explores here has to do with the relation between an

individual and God. Is that relation based on works of
law or on faith? This question can be asked entirely
apart from the history of God's dealings with his people
Israel; it is, indeed, almost ahistorical. The time of
works and the time of faith take place not in God's
historical acts but within the individual. In anyone's life
there are two existential possibilities — an existence
that relies on works of law (and seeks to stand before
God on the basis of its own claims), or an existence
that believes God's announcement of acceptance.

Central to understanding this first way of thinking
is the reference to Abraham in 3:6-9. Abraham believed
God. What sort of trust was his? Our first reaction
might be to say that he trusted God's *promise*, but Paul
does not use that language here. He says: to Abraham
the gospel was preached. God was not simply promising
Abraham that in due time something would be done
for Abraham. He was preaching gospel to Abraham —
announcing the good news of his gracious acceptance.
"So, then, those who are men of faith are blessed with
Abraham who had faith" (3:9). This appears to be a
quite general possibility: Human beings are made for
the God from whom they are estranged, and this God
is able to address their anxiety-ridden, yet hopeful,
existence. Wherever and whenever God speaks to them
a word of acceptance, the gospel is preached to anxious
human hearts and "children of Abraham" may respond
in faith.

When, however, Paul turns again to the story of
Abraham in 3:15ff., the emphasis is far more objective
than subjective, more historical than existential. Having first introduced Abraham to show that one is justified only by faith rather than by 'works of law', Paul
moves into a quite different argument delimiting the
time of the 'law' by reference to Abraham and his seed.
No longer is Paul's concern with 'works of law' done
by an anxious conscience; 'law' is now clearly the Old
Testament law given to Israel. And a new word, 'prom-

ise', now functions as a replacement for 'gospel'. That word, though natural enough in the context of the Abraham story, had not appeared in 3:6-9. But from 3:13-4:31 it occupies a position of prominence. Even the meaning of *faith* seems to shift. No longer does it mean primarily the trust of an individual; instead, it is almost interchangeable with Christ himself, the one who brings the time of faith (3:23-26). The *law* is now clearly the Old Testament law, limited to a particular time and understood as a power under which human beings once lived (so that God might accomplish his purposes in history). And *faith* has become the time of Christ, when the law is no longer needed because the promise has been fulfilled. In this section of Galatians, the time of law and the time of faith are not within the individual but are played out in the history of God's deeds of promise and fulfillment.[33]

Either way of speaking can constitute a mode of entry for the Christian message. Both ways are governed by the contours of biblical narrative—the first by the sketch of human existence given in the primeval history of the opening eleven chapters of Genesis, the second by the scheme of promise/fulfillment that Christians have discerned in the two testaments. But the first of these ways, which takes up some of the concerns of Cartesian theology, may be more readily accessible and significant for those whose understanding of human life is not shaped by Israel's story, who have never learned to say, "A wandering Aramean was my father, . . . and the LORD brought us out of Egypt with a mighty hand and an outstretched arm" (Deut. 26:5, 8). Even those who make no such confession may still come to understand our life as estranged from and yet sustained by the power of God—banished from the garden, but clothed and allowed to live. Christians may speak to such fundamental concerns of human experience even while simultaneously exploring the rich grammar of their way of life and seeking to hand it on.

Indeed, precisely as we emphasize that the Bible—though many of its parts are not great works of art—tells a story, we will look for ways to do justice to both Cartesian and non-Cartesian concerns. This story, mythic in its sweep and dimensions, narrates the reality within which we live, but it does so in ways that call the imagination into play and shed a numinous light on our existence. Good readers or hearers of this story will not always be alike.

In *Cymbeline*, one of Shakespeare's late dramatic romances, there is a scene that suggests two ways of reading or hearing a story.[34] Belarius, an old man who has brought up the king's two sons, explains how he used to tell stories to the boys and how each would respond to the telling. Of the older boy, Polydore, Belarius says:

> When on my three-foot stool I sit and tell
> The war-like feats I have done, his spirits fly out
> Into my story: say, "Thus mine enemy fell,
> And thus I set my foot on's neck;" even then
> The princely blood flows in his cheek, he sweats,
> Strains his young nerves, and puts himself in posture
> That acts my words.[35]

The younger boy, Cadwal,

> in as like a figure,
> Strikes life into my speech and shows much more
> His own conceiving.[36]

Both boys respond to the stories, but in quite different ways. Polydore is the model of Thielicke's non-Cartesian theologian: his spirits fly out into the story. He places himself into the narrative, lives within it, permits it to define his world, and acts it out. What he is, the story determines. The younger brother, Cadwal, has about him the Cartesian air. Hearing a story, he strikes life into it "and shows much more his own conceiving." He responds to the story not just as a tale to be faithfully enacted but as a story with significant meaning

for his present experience. Imaginatively re-creating
the story by responding to it out of his own concerns,
he strikes life into it.

If we believe that the Christian message really is a
great drama, we will not wish that there should be no
Cadwals among us. To be sure, they bring a special set
of dangers. If sometimes they strike life into the speech,
they may as often find in it little more than their own
conceiving. And when that happens, the story itself
cannot transform our existence. We are in need then
of the Polydores, the skilled grammarians of the Christian way of life. Or, if we are especially favored, we
may on occasion find Cadwal and Polydore rolled into
one. Thus, for example, St. Augustine, who (in *City of
God*) set human life within the world of biblical narrative and (in his *Confessions*) read that narrative in
the light of his own experience and unforgettably
struck life into its message.

VI. Whither?

Perhaps we are now in a position to "trump" Alasdair MacIntyre's suggestion that we await a new St.
Benedict. It may be that, especially in this time and
place, we await a new St. Augustine! If this raises the
stakes to a still more imposing level, it may nevertheless be a useful way to think about what Christian
ethics needs at the present time. For we need more
than a way to carve out a distinctively Christian life
amidst the ruins of a surrounding civilization; we need
also some way to maintain contact with all that is good
in that civilization, to understand that if it is often
vicious (in the technical, moral sense), its vice is, at
least sometimes, "splendid."

Augustine was elevated to the See of Hippo in the
year the Emperor Theodosius died. It was Theodosius
who had really accomplished what is often charged to

Constantine's account: made the temporal power sub-
ordinate to the spiritual and found in the defense of
the church a new principle for political cohesion within
the empire. For that reason Charles Norris Cochrane
wrote that it was Theodosius who "crossed the divide
which separates the ancient from the medieval world."[37]
But it might seem, then, as if Augustine were the
wrong guide for our time and place. At a time when —
so we are told — we are experiencing the last gasps of
a once-Christian civilization and turning to a post-
Christian world, what could be gained from turning to
one who stood at the beginning of the development of
that Christian world and was, in fact, one of its chief
architects? Only this: that to live in a time of transition
and upheaval as Augustine did, in a world partly Chris-
tianized but in large part pagan, is to live in a time
much like ours. *We* know that the historical momentum
of Augustine's time was to eventuate in a Christian
world. *He* did not. As a result, he sought only to make
sense of his world, to find in it what meaning he could,
to praise it wherever possible — but not to let the Christian life be definitively shaped by it. "In a world, the
moral and intellectual foundations of which appeared
to have been shattered, he clung doggedly to a faith
that, however 'vicious' or defective in principle, the
secular effort of mankind had not been wholly in vain;
and he was determined not to resign himself, like so
many of his contemporaries, to the cult of futility."[38]

In his mature work, especially the great *City of God*,
Augustine accomplished this by envisioning the natural
realm and the whole of human history — the *saeculum* —
within the narrative of the Bible. Not because God acts
only within some separate "sacred history" or community, but because this story alone can give us a clue
to the divine purpose within the *saeculum*.[39] This approach gave Augustine a new vantage point for thinking about the Christian life within our world. No longer
compelled to choose either a Eusebian reading of his-

tory which sought to portray God's activity as the meaning of secular history, or a sectarian view which could not see the natural world as in any sense the theater of God's action, Augustine discerned a more enduring tension.[40] Two cities forever in conflict — and any actual community a tension between the two, a constant swaying to and fro between these ultimate possibilities. And the lesson is there for us also to learn. Since the church is not *the* City of God, it cannot sustain its own way of life. It can only and always be some portion of the world, suffering the transformations effected by divine grace, on the way. And since the world is not *the* earthly city, the splendor of its vice must be affirmed even while the church during its earthly sojourn attends, quite self-consciously, with special care to its own way of life.

2. Human Nature: The Human Being

> how sweet is love itself possessed,
> When but love's shadows are so rich in joy!
> Shakespeare, *Romeo and Juliet*

When, in the story told in Genesis 3, sin enters the world, the life of human beings is dramatically altered. They hide from God. They are set at odds with each other, unable to acknowledge their partnership in sin. They are faced with rebellion by the co-creation: pain in childbearing and in the toil which sustains life. By pointing us to what should have been — or, better, what continues to exist by virtue of God's creative world, even if it exists only in a broken and distorted condition — this story suggests three angles of vision from which to think about human nature. Each is captured in a preposition:[1]

(1) Human beings stand *before* God, hearing the divine address and made for life in harmony with God.

(2) Human beings stand *beside* each other, addressed by God not in isolation but in the community of male and female.

(3) Human beings stand *over* the co-creation, addressed by God as those responsible for its care.

These prepositional bonds remind us of the central spheres of life in which we are called to faithfulness:

the political community — in which all are equal because all are addressed by God and whose limit is found precisely in the fact that its citizens are addressed by One who is greater than the sovereign; the marital bond — in which, paradigmatically, the love that reflects God's being is shared; the sphere of work — in which the co-creation is offered back to God. Our concern here, however, is with the larger contours of our life — human beings in relation to the co-creation, the Creator, and each other.

I. The Environment of Human Beings

"I believe that God has made me and all creatures. . . ." With that "existential" affirmation Martin Luther began his explanation of the first article of the creed in his *Small Catechism.* "The simple piety of this statement," George Hendry has written, "conceals a presumptuous impiety, for it makes it appear that the entire furniture of creation has been put there for my sake."[2] Whether this is the correct way to read Luther may perhaps be doubted. His German text reads: "Ich glaube, dass mich Gott geschaffen hat samt allen Kreaturen. . . ." And the Latin captures the same emphasis: "Credo, quod Deus creaverit me, una cum omnibus creaturis. . . ." "I believe that God has created me, together with all creatures. . . ."[3]

Whatever the correct interpretation of Luther may be, the issue raised is important. Even to speak of "the environment of human beings" may seem to focus too exclusively on humanity. The created world becomes simply a backdrop against which the human drama is played out, or a resource needed by us as we pursue our purposes in history. Of course, we need not look only to theological views to find reflected such a view of nature. We may wonder, for example, whether much of our ecological concern is not primarily a concern for

the habitation of human beings, a concern for our species.[4] And there is more than a little irony in the fact
that our age, so concerned to understand our kinship
with the natural world, should in other contexts be
eager to define the nature of the human person in ways
which take little account of the body. There are countless ways, not just theological ones, in which nature
may cease to be the co-creation.

We need not, however, fear unduly the charge of
anthropocentrism. Properly understood, a special concern for humanity is appropriate within a theocentric
faith, the true opposite of which might be termed cos-
mocentrism. Indeed, the movement of Israelite faith
was precisely *away* from the mother-goddess, from a
religious attitude which could not clearly distinguish
between God, humanity, and the natural world, and
which experienced union of human and divine through
the cycles of nature or the fecund powers of generation.
Israel wanted to be different.

> Our God is in the heavens;
>   he does whatever he pleases.
> Their idols are silver and gold,
>   the work of men's hands.[6]
>   (Psalm 115:3-4)

The world from which Israelite faith distinguished itself was one in which experience of the inner order of
the cosmos was itself union with the divine. We may
adapt an image of Owen Barfield's and say that the
natural world was not a resource or a stage but like a
garment worn. To wear it properly, not to separate the
inner and outer self, was to be one with the deity.[5]

When Israel's theocentric faith turned in another
direction, it did not envision the creation simply as a
backdrop for human action. That was part of the truth,
but only a part.

> Thou dost cause the grass to grow for the cattle,
>   and plants for man to cultivate,

> that he may bring forth food from the earth,
>   and wine to gladden the heart of man,
> oil to make his face shine,
>   and bread to strengthen man's heart.
> The trees of the LORD are watered abundantly,
>   the cedars of Lebanon which he planted.
> In them the birds build their nests;
>   the stork has her home in the fir trees.
> The high mountains are for the wild goats;
>   the rocks are a refuge for the badgers.
>   (Psalm 104:14-18)

The badgers and the wild goats are not forgotten! The natural world serves human life but does not exist for that purpose alone. Still, within this theocentric vision the *anthropos* has a special role to play. In Genesis 1 dominion is given to humankind. In that same story it is clear that the praise of God is to resound through the creation. "And God saw everything that he had made, and behold it was very good." Human beings are priests of creation, called to exercise dominion by offering back to God what he has given for their sustenance. And they are stewards, given responsibility to care for the co-creation. If the world were only "nature"—a self-enclosed and self-contained organism living and growing of itself—human dominion could only mean mastery of the world, a mastery exercised by those who experienced themselves as rational wills. But if the world is "creation," human dominion must mean stewardship and priesthood in a world that is not ours to possess. From this perspective environmental ethics must offer more than endless discussions of our obligations to future generations. It must reflect upon the virtues—humility, gratitude, trust, moderation, contentment—which are needed in the present moment for a proper care of the earth. Perhaps the greatest contribution Christians could make to care for the environment would be a renewed determination to keep the holy day holy. If, entrusting ourselves to the keeping of God, we were really to give up our attempts at mastery of the co-creation on Sunday, who can predict what consequences for environmental ethics might follow?

Thus, the way to a right understanding of the co-creation does not lie back in the pagan image of the world as a garment we wear, an image shattered for Christians by Israel's attack upon idolatry. Nor is the right image that which arises from thinking not of creation but of nature — a stage on which human life is displayed. Instead, nature must be imaged as "a ship, of which we are the crew, and which it is our responsibility to navigate to its destination."[6] If such a view is anthropocentric, it is equally theocentric. It understands the co-creation as given by God to serve human life — but not given solely for that end. Mary Midgley has accurately described this way of thinking.

> The idea that things are *there* for some external purpose seems to need a theological context, and this view did of course grow out of one. But that context will not subjugate everything to man. Certainly Judaeo-Christian thinking made the human race much more central than many other religions do, but it still considered man to be God's steward. Divine aims were always paramount, and God had created all his creatures for his own purposes, not for man's. Non-human beings count in this picture as having their own special value. Redwoods and pythons, frogs, moles and albatrosses are not failed humans or early tryouts for humans or tools put there to advance human development.[7]

A proper dominion must include, therefore, both a recognition that we rightly use the co-creation to sustain and enrich our life *and* an unwillingness to regard the earth *simply* as a resource to be spent in the interest of our species. Understanding ourselves to have been placed *over* the co-creation, we should see that dominion cannot mean domination.

Thus, an anthropocentric theme is grounded in the theocentric vision of biblical narrative. By contrast, the cosmocentric vision that dominates our age teaches us to regard all life, including our own, as essentially the same. From this perspective we can justify using other animals and natural resources to serve human well-being only from a frankly self-interested premise. "We sacrifice other species to our own not because our own has any objective metaphysical privilege over others, but simply because it is ours."[8] And why, we may wonder, if the stronger and more rational animals may use the weaker and less rational to serve their needs, should not the stronger and more rational humans use the weaker in similar ways? That no reason may be found is beginning to become evident — in our treatment, for example, of fetuses, the mentally retarded, and the senile. How much better would not a frank recognition of human dominion be: a dominion not of nature but of the co-creation, a dominion exercised by those who are to be stewards and priests of that co-creation? Why, after all, should a dominion exercised by the strong and gifted over those who are weak and without special abilities be thought morally superior to a dominion exercised by humankind over the co-creation — and exercised *for no reason other than* the command of God? We may and must use the earth in service of human life. But the justification for this dominion is not grounded in our superior power or reason; its warrant lies simply in the will of God who so orders his creation. Understanding our responsibility in this way we may be less likely to put on airs or imagine ourselves immune to mistakes. And we will have taken at least a small step in the direction of learning to use the creation as stewards who care for it and priests who offer it back to God with glad hearts. That is the rightful dominion of human beings, who stand *over* the co-creation.

II. The Human Person

As creatures called by God to exercise responsibility for the co-creation, humans experience themselves as strangely two-sided beings. The earth for which we are made responsible is the co-creation, and like it we are finite. But we are called to responsibility by the address of God, and we therefore freely transcend the finite world and are made for life in harmony with God. This vision of human nature informs the story in Genesis 2 of the creation of humankind: "the LORD God formed man of dust from the ground, and breathed into his nostrils the breath of life; and man became a living being." Present in that verse in compressed form is an understanding of human beings as both (a) rooted in nature and history (formed of the dust of the ground), and (b) self-aware and able to transcend to some extent natural and historical necessity (given the divine breath of life). It is always possible to try to reduce our nature to either its material or its spiritual dimension, but such reductionisms cannot capture the complexity that is a human person. We are embodied persons and personalized bodies — and to understand human nature in this way is the task of Christian thought.

The jargon which has become common currency for describing such a view is that of the human person as a "psychophysical unity": not a compound of two simpler entities which can exist whole and entire in isolation, but an irreducible unity. Thus, religiously, we would not speak of the soul as if it were the real person and the body only its garment or vehicle. Put philosophically, we are enjoined to avoid Cartesian notions of the mind as a "ghost" inhabiting the "machine" of the body. What sometimes results, however, is an entirely functional understanding of human personhood. The person is described simply as a body capable of intentional action. To speak of the "spiritual" side of our nature — that about us which is not simply body and which cannot be adequately described by reference to position, movement, and shape—is to speak of certain characteristic functions or capacities.[9]

This raises, however, the question of the "person" who lacks such characteristics. And even if there are satisfactory ways to handle the very old question whether a person sleeping is still a person, it may prove more difficult on this view to ascribe personhood to fetuses, infants and (even) young children, the senile, and the irreversibly comatose. Thus, for example, in an important work in bioethics which gathers together many strands of a view becoming increasingly common, H. Tristram Engelhardt asserts that those who count for the most morally are not all human beings but only persons. And persons are those who can be "concerned about moral arguments and . . . convinced by them." They must be self-conscious, rational, free to choose, and must possess moral concern.[10] It is at once clear that many human beings will not qualify for personhood on such grounds, and our obligations to those humans who do not qualify will be less stringent than to those— like ourselves!—who are self-conscious, rational, and in control. Englehardt does not hesitate, for example, to speak of parents as owning their children, at least until such time as the "entity" becomes self-conscious. "One . . . owns what one produces. One might think here of animals and young children."[11]

I suggest, however, that this increasingly popular understanding tears asunder the two aspects of our nature—makes a dualism out of the duality that characterizes us. In Shakespeare's *Cymbeline* there is a scene in which the queen is gathering poisons. With her is Cornelius, an upright physician who suspects the evil deeds she plans. She, however, claims to intend nothing more than a few experiments.

QUEEN
I will try the forces
Of these thy compounds on such creatures as

We count not worth the hanging—but none human—
To try the vigor of them and apply
Allayments to their act, and by them gather
Their several virtues and effects.
                    CORNELIUS
                                    Your Highness
Shall from this practice but make hard your heart.[12]

Versions of Cornelius's argument are common in contemporary discussions of personhood. Thus, for example, having claimed that infants are not persons and
are therefore not entitled to protection and care equal
to that which we owe each other, Engelhardt nevertheless suggests that we might wish to treat them
almost as if they were. Such a practice would support
"virtues such as sympathy and care for human life,
especially when that life is fragile and defenseless."[13]
Sometimes the argument is put more negatively: If we
falter in our care for human beings who do not rise to
the level of personhood, we may become hardened and
calloused even in our treatment of those who do.

Inevitably there is something a little disturbing
about such arguments—suggesting as they do that the
chief reason to care for "subpersonal" lives is the results for our own character or the effect that failing to
do so might have on lives like our own. Moreover, these
claims are hardly persuasive as specimens of argument.
One might as easily suppose that once we make a clear
distinction between personal and subpersonal forms of
life, even the most cruel treatment of the latter need
have no deleterious effect on our care for the former.
We may become increasingly calloused in our care for
subpersonal (animal and human) life, but there is no
logical reason why that need affect the way we treat
human beings (or other creatures) who have risen to
the level of personhood. Thus, the argument is not rationally compelling. If, nevertheless, we feel its force,
the reason is hard to account for in terms of a theory
like Engelhardt's. We feel our kinship with human

beings who are neither rational nor self-conscious, feel that what we do to them might affect the way we treat each other, because we share with them our embodied condition. We too are not just free, rational spirits but are finite beings—living organisms whose characteristic pattern of activity is to some extent given, immune to direct intentional modification.[14] The issue, therefore, is not simply one of obligations or rights. At stake is the development and enlargement within our lives of virtues like sympathy and compassion. Nor is this simply a point about private morality which can or should be separated from the public sphere (where, we will be told, only questions or rights or duties are relevant). What sort of people we wish to be, what the boundaries of our community are, what virtues we wish to foster in our common life—these are public, political questions.

That we can feel the force of an argument which worries about practices that may make hard our hearts suggests a second consideration: There may be deeper theoretical difficulties with the distinction between personal and subpersonal forms of human life. There is a difference between (a) distinguishing characteristics of the human species, and (b) qualifications for membership in that species. It may be that among the distinguishing characteristics of humanity are features like rationality, self-consciousness, and moral concern. Nevertheless, one can belong to the human species without exercising (or even having the capacity to exercise) such characteristics. To belong to humankind one need not exercise its distinguishing traits; one need only be begotten of human parents. Why, then, would we let personal qualities count morally for so much more than membership in humankind? I alluded earlier to one possible reason when discussing human beings in relation to the co-creation: We contract our spirit of concern to those who are stronger and more gifted, those most like ourselves. Another reason now suggests itself as well. We may not have fully eliminated from our thinking the ghost in the machine — the sense that the body is no more than a vehicle for that free personal spirit who really counts. We need constantly to be reminded that it is embodied human beings who are addressed by the word and call of God — made, that is, in his image.

Indeed, for Christians the concept of "personhood" cannot help but be a theological one. A person is not a kind or sort of thing, one having certain "personal" capacities. A person is an irreplaceable self — someone who has a history. We might say: not that we are able to be addessed, but that God addresses us and calls us to himself, constitutes us as persons. Here, in what we say about human nature and not only in what we say about the justification of sinners, we must honor the initiative of God, who bestows dignity upon us in his very commitment to us.[15]

In several recent writings Oliver O'Donovan has called attention to other theological underpinnings of a proper notion of personhood.[16] When Christians need-ed to find ways to speak of the one person of Christ (with both divine and human natures) and of the one God who was Father, Son, and Spirit, they were forced to give close attention to the concept of a person. And the understanding of a person at which they arrived was set in opposition to any characterization of per-sonhood in terms of qualities or capacities.

The Greek word *hypostasis* and the Latin *persona* were used to refer to the three persons within the unity of the Godhead. A *hypostasis* was a reality underlying all characteristics or qualities. A *persona* was the char-acter's mask in the theater — hence, an appearance of an individual, an appearance having continuity within the story of the character's appearances. "When one spoke of a 'person' one spoke of these different, suc-cessive, and changing appearances as one connected appearance; when one spoke of 'hypostasis' one spoke of something that underlay them all and so made them one, the hidden thread of individual existence.... "[17] And when affirming belief in Christ's one person (with two natures), Christians wished to say neither that he was really two persons (having two sets of "personal" characteristics) nor that in his one person some human characteristics had been displaced by divine ones. His individual identity could not be formulated in terms of personal capacities or characteristics. Rather, he was, quite simply, an individual with a history. In that history he acquires and displays various personal qualities, but he is not one with them. They do not make him a person. The Christian conclusion about what it meant to be a person followed straightforwardly: "Personality *discloses* personhood; it does not constitute it."[18] The mystery of the human person — the mystery of one addressed by and freely destined for God — cannot be captured in any set of personal qualities. The person is simply a "someone who" — a someone with a history.[19]

If this is what it means to be a person, an obvious question faces us: How shall we locate or come to know persons if we are not to identify their personal existence with possession of certain qualities? And the answer is clear. If a person is a "someone who," a someone with a history, we can know him or her only by entering into that history, only by personal engagement and commitment — or what Christians have called love. To ask in advance for a list of characteristics by which to identify those whom we are to love is to begin in precisely the wrong place. It is to begin with a question whose answer will almost surely constrict our sympathies to those like ourselves — and thereby limit the scope of our love. The first question is never whether the other human being is someone who merits our loving commitment by virtue of his or her characteristics; the first question is whether we are willing to extend such love.[20]

To whom is such commitment properly given? If we keep in mind the duality of our nature — the truth that the free personal spirit is always conjoined with the finite earthly body — the answer will be: this commitment should be given to all who bear the human form, all who are begotten of human parents. For example, discussing how we learn to value children who are born retarded, William F. May has noted that parents "bond" to such children not because of any natural capacities possessed by the children but simply because of the givenness of the relation. These children are "creatures whose being and worth disclose themselves chiefly in the context of ties."[21] If we do not tie ourselves to them in a common history, no bond is formed and no value disclosed. And more generally, it is surely the experience of most parents that they must first commit themselves to their children in an ongoing history together if they are to recognize in them personal beings like themselves. The notion that such commitment is appropriate only if we have first recognized the person in the child (or, even, the fetus) cannot account for the necessities of child-rearing. Such notions must be inadequate, must fail to comprehend the mystery of the human person, since they fail to understand a person as someone who is addressed by God, called within our finite, embodied existence to answer to God — and they fail, therefore, to invite us to enter in love into a history that precedes our own discernment of the person and may continue even when the living person has passed beyond the reach of our words. This must be said if we are to understand the human person who stands *before* God.

III. Community in Love

No human being stands in isolation before God and over the co-creation; rather we stand beside each other,

created for community in love. The creation of human
beings as male and female establishes for humanity a
task: those who are different must come to know themselves as humankind—sharers in a community which
neither obliterates nor underplays their differences.
The task cannot be simply to establish oneness, as if
the differences of our finite locations and embodied
condition were of no significance. Yet the task must be
possible, since we are also free spirits who transcend
our particular locations and are able to stand *beside*
each other.

Our task is nothing less than this: to achieve within
human life the love that is a dim reflection of the life
of God. In the Triune God—Father as initiating ground,
Son as coequal respondent, and Spirit as the mutual
bond which springs from their giving and receiving—
we have a picture of love. God, therefore, is not simply
being, but also activity: the activity of giving and receiving, of mutual love. If we reflect upon this picture
of union in love, we will find in it three aspects which
must be present in any love that has come to full fruition: (1) An affirmation of and delight in the sheer fact
of the other's existence is present in the Father's be-
getting of the Son—and this we may call 'benevolence'
or 'good will'. (2) A union of affections is present in the
Son's response to the Father's gift—and this we may
call 'reciprocity' or 'mutuality' in love. (3) Permeating
and interpenetrating the Father's affirmation of the
Son and the Son's glad response is a *self-giving* Spirit
that leads the Father to give all that is his, and the
Son to be a willing recipient. Love involves both benevolence and mutuality—and underlying each must
be a self-giving spirit. This love, present first and fully
in the life of God, is to be imaged in our lives.

Because, however, we are creatures both free and
finite, the image of divine love in our life must be suited
to our created condition. We are finite—located in a
particular time and place, bound to certain people in

bonds of special affection and attachment. We are free — able to some extent to move beyond these limits, to enlarge our sympathies and learn to love anyone who bears the human form. This raises the question of particularity or preference in love. We are finite — needy beings with desires that must be met if we are to attain any happiness or fulfillment. And we are free — able to some extent to put ourselves in the other's place and seek his happiness even in preference to our own. This raises the question of self-love.[22]

The problem of preference in love is nicely posed in a passage from Calvin's *Institutes.*

> Now since Christ has shown in the parable of the Samaritan that the term "neighbor" includes even the most remote person, we are not expected to limit the precept of love to those in close relationships. I do not deny that the more closely a man is linked to us, the more intimate obligation we have to assist him. It is the common habit of mankind that the more closely men are bound together by ties of kinship, of acquaintance, or of neighborhood, the more responsibilities for one another they share. This does not offend God; for his providence, as it were, leads us to it. But I say: we ought to embrace the whole human race without exception in a single feeling of love; here there is no distinction between barbarian and Greek, worthy and unworthy, friend and enemy, since all should be contemplated in God, not in themselves.[23]

That the issue is not an easy one is evident in the way Calvin's thought swings back and forth within this short passage. He begins with the claim that love is not to be limited and that we are to love "even the most remote person." But he grants at once that we commonly think ourselves obligated more to some than to others. So far is he from denying the fact of such special obligations that he ascribes them to God's providential ordering of the creation. But, having made this admission, he at once returns to his first affirmation: "we ought to embrace the whole human race without exception in a single feeling of love." Evidently we need both forms of love—special attachment to those who stand in close relationship to us and a more universal neighbor-love that is open-hearted and receptive to all.

The close attachments built upon special loyalties and preferences are essential to our lives. Since we are personalized bodies, such special attachments—to time, place, and particular people—are integral to our happiness. A love lacking particular attachments must inevitably seem to lack warmth and intimacy—to lack something essential to any love that has come to its full fruition. It is equally true, though, that, taken by themselves, partial and preferential loves may seem to lack something just as essential to any perfected love. What this "something" is was captured nicely by Kierkegaard in one of his short parables.

> Suppose there were two artists, and the one said, "I have travelled much and seen much in the world, but I have sought in vain to find a man worth painting. I have found no face with such perfection of beauty that I could make up my mind to paint it. In every face I have seen one or another little fault. Therefore I seek in vain." Would this indicate that this artist was a great artist? On the other hand, the second one said, "Well, I do not pretend to be a real artist; neither have I travelled in foreign lands. But remaining in the little circle of men who are closest to me, I have not found a face so insignificant or so full of faults that I still could not discern in it a more beautiful side and discover something glorious. Therefore I am happy in the art I practice." Would this not indicate that precisely this one was the artist, one who by bringing a certain something with him found then and there what the much-travelled artist did not find anywhere in the world, perhaps because he did not bring a certain something with him! Consequently the second of the two was the artist.[24]

And so, Kierkegaard remarks in the same context, love means "bringing it along oneself"—bringing the spirit that affirms the sheer existence of the other, not simply the spirit that is drawn to those with characteristics that hold promise of a warm and reciprocal relationship.

That both loves — particular attachment and sheer affirmation of another — are necessary should be no surprise, since both are included in the picture of perfected love given in the triune life of God. It is not easy, though, as Calvin clearly recognized, for us to manage the intricate simultaneities of a life including both. There have been perhaps four general strategies used by Christians in their attempts to hold together both loves within the Christian life.[25]

One strategy is to connect the two loves closely, but without attempting to derive either from the other. From this perspective we would simply note that benevolence and mutuality are two different forms of love — but connected when we permit the former to act as a limit and check upon the latter. That is, benevolence is taken to be chiefly a negative principle, setting limits to what we may do to anyone. Within those limits we are free to pursue our particular attachments and loves. As long as we do neither harm nor injustice to any neighbor, we need not worry about giving ourselves in the special bonds to which the providence of God leads us. This is a useful strategy, one which has certainly been very common in Christian practice, attractive because of its realism and common sense. Its danger though is complacency; for it seems to miss the active and positive character of love, the way in which love strains to overcome boundaries which separate human beings from one another. The danger of this strategy is that it permits us all too easily to answer as the young man did when Jesus pointed him to the commandments: "All these have I kept from my youth."

A second strategy is to begin with benevolence — with a love that embraces every human being. Making it fundamental in our understanding of love, we may then try to build down from it by incorporating within

its scope particular loves. They will be understood simply as specifications or particular applications of our
benevolence. The argument is likely to proceed from
consideration of our finitude. Our benevolence can be
exercised toward all in the sense that we can pray for
all, have good will for all, and be ready to receive the
many who cross our path. But since we are finite, this
benevolence will in practice have to be expressed most
fully toward certain people near and dear to us. Thus
distinctions in love are still permitted: We love some
people with special attachment, but we love them as
we would love all if we could—with a love of benevolence, not preference. What is impressive about this
strategy is the way in which it tries to learn with full
seriousness the lesson in Kierkegaard's parable of the
two artists: that a love which looks for particular, lovable characteristics may never find anyone to love. The
weakness of this approach, however, is that it can affirm
the created limits of human life only with great difficulty. If special attachments were really nothing more
than specifications of general benevolence, they should
be almost random in their occurrence. But in fact they
are built upon preferred qualifications and characteristics. Begin with benevolence, add the truth that as
finite beings we cannot enter into special relations with
more than a few people, and we can arrive at a justification for being friends with some rather than with
all the world. But we are unlikely to justify being
friends with any particular man or woman for the sorts
of reasons friends give. They are not chosen at random
as this second strategy requires—and they are not because such an understanding of attachment is ill suited
to beings who are not simply free spirits transcending
every particular affection.

Instead of trying to build down from benevolence to
special bonds of mutual love, we may reverse the direction of movement. A third strategy is to build up
from our particular attachments to a more universal

benevolence. Thus, I marry my wife not because my love for her is a specification of some more universal regard for neighbors but because I am drawn to her in particular. But having committed myself to her, attempting to care for her well-being in particular, I may gradually become a person more ready to care for the good of any neighbor. The philosopher J. L. Stocks captured such movement in a lovely story about a little six-year-old girl who had received a bicycle as a gift from another girl who had outgrown it. When she knew the bicycle was to be hers, no doubt after a considerable period of desiring a bike of her own, she addressed to the bicycle a short but memorable poem.

O beautiful bike, I love you so:
It is so nice to see you go.
I will wash you and clean you and take you home—
O beautiful bike, will you come?[26]

How striking is the poem's last line! The little girl's desire to possess the bike, to have it be hers, to give it special care and attention—all that is transformed into an appreciative love that simply delights in the bicycle's existence and grants it a kind of independence. The poem captures in brief compass the movement we are asked to make in life when we understand our special bonds as schools in which we are taught the beginnings of a more universal love. It is true, however, that for this third strategy the compatibility of the two forms of love must be left largely to faith rather than sight. No quick transformation is promised or anticipated.

Finally, we should note a fourth strategy, although it is not precisely an attempt to hold special attachments together with universal love in a single life. Noting that there is a third element besides benevolence and mutuality in the picture of perfected love in the life of God, we might argue that the most fundamental element in love is a spirit of self-giving. If we make it fundamental in Christian life, we get what can be called a Franciscan understanding of love. Without denying the importance of special attachments for finite, embodied human beings, and without questioning the necessity of universal neighbor-love, this strategy recognizes that at least some Christians may seek to enact the more fundamental rhythm of self-giving which makes the divine life possible—and to do so without asking whether it is equivalent to general benevolence or whether it leads to the inner reciprocities of mutual love. The power of this way of life lies in the passion of its self-spending, but it is perhaps better described as a special calling of some than as a strategy for holding together benevolence and mutuality within the movement of a single life.

It is too simple a stereotype—but, like most stereotypes, in some measure true—to say that the first two strategies have dominated Protestant thought and the last two have more often been dominant in the Catholic understanding of life. It has, in particular, been the genius of Catholicism to combine the third and fourth strategies—to recognize that for most of us, pilgrims toward rest in God, the necessary movement is one that builds up from particular attachments to benevolence, but that there may be some who are called to live even now as if particular and partial loves were no longer essential in human life. The combination is an alluring one—impressive in practice and persuasive in theory.

The question of justifying special attachments—of preferring one human being to another—is a central issue in our understanding of love. But equally important is the choice between self and anyone else. One way to approach this question is to suppose that life regularly and normally presents us with choices between our own welfare and that of others. If we picture life in this way—and certainly to the degree that it is this way—there can be little doubt what Christians must do. The neighbor must be loved, even at great cost to ourselves; for we know that we are eternally secure with God. This is how we ought to understand the commandment to love the neighbor as we love ourselves. It is not a recommendation of neighbor-love *in addition* to self-love. It simply recognizes that we *do* usually love ourselves — and, since we do, we are commanded to take that love of self as a standard or model for how to love others. We affirm and delight in our own existence; we seek our own well-being. And we should learn to say of others as we do of ourselves: "it's good that you exist."[27]

It is not fully satisfactory, however, to picture life as a choice between self-love and neighbor-love. Many women, for example, have come to think of Christian love as simply a requirement that they give themselves to the service of others. We need to distinguish between a love that in its *nature* is self-referential and a love that has the self for its *object*. Not all our loves are or need be pure benevolence, sheer affirmation of the existence of another. Many of them are related to our own desires for satisfaction and completion. These are self-referential, but their object need not be the self. Their form is: "The self seeks its good in. . . ." We may seek our good in friendship, marriage, learning, service, contemplation, artistry, play, work. But the simple fact that we seek our own good does not make ours the forbidden love of self. A world in which no one pursued his own projects and desires would be a dead world. No one's good could be served; indeed, we might have difficulty even knowing what the good of another person was.

What is forbidden Christians is not such self-referential love but, rather, making the self the object of our love. "The self seeks its good *in the self*." Pursuit of our own projects and undertakings is not prohibited. What is forbidden is that we should take as our aim in acting the integrated fulfillment over time of *all* our

interests and desires; for such an aim would exclude
from life the possibility of commitments to others
which, when taken seriously, would themselves make
such an aim impossible.[28] If we begin to make our self
the object of our love, we will quickly find that many
desires and projects which are quite natural for us will
have to be stifled; for they require that we focus upon
someone or something outside the self. A man may seek
his good in loving a woman. But in doing so he will
have to take *her* as the object of his love. And this, in
turn, will inevitably require the sacrifice of some of his
other desires and goals. If he is unwilling to make that
sacrifice, he cannot seek his good in loving her — one
who is other than himself.

Such an understanding of love sees us as we really
are — needy creatures who depend upon each other for
protection, fulfillment, and flourishing. Yet, it takes a
certain effort of the imagination really to think of this
on a large scale. Lewis Hyde has used examples of gift
exchanges in tribal societies to explore such interde-
pendence. Gift exhanges — in which the gift is received
and given again, though not returned to the original
giver — illustrate "circular" rather than simply "reciprocal" giving. "[W]hen the gift moves in a circle no one
ever receives it from the same person he gives it to. . . .
When I give to someone from whom I do not receive
(and yet I do receive elsewhere) it is as if the gift goes
around a corner before it comes back. I have to give
blindly."[29] In doing this I may seem insufficiently attentive to my own fulfillment — and, of course, it is
always possible that the exchange may break down and
no return ever come my way. But in the providence of
God "[t]he gift . . . moves toward the empty place. . . .
Our generosity may leave us empty, but our emptiness
then pulls gently at the whole until the thing in motion
returns to fill us up again."[30] When this happens, we
flourish — and in our complex, developed societies this
may happen far more often than we imagine or have

eyes to see. And if it fails to happen? Then we face the moment in which sacrifice is called for and love must hope in God alone.

However often life may present us with the necessity of choosing between our own good and that of another, we should not deny that the self's good comes from attention to others and may rightly be sought there. For this is how God cares for us. "The courtesy of the Emperor has absolutely decreed that no man can paddle his own canoe and every man can paddle his fellow's. . . ."[31] Thus, in practice it may be almost impossible to specify where joy in someone else's good begins and desire for our own good stops. Only a far too introspective conscience would suppose that the distinction was ours rather than God's to make. All we can say is that in the perfected life of love that is God there is spontaneous self-giving, affirmation of the other, and glad receptivity.

Life *beside* our fellow human beings must be a community in love — paddling another's canoe while ours is moved along by the efforts of still others. This is, in fact, the very rhythm of the divine life, a rhythm we are called to learn, a rhythm God has enacted also in our history: "He saved others; himself he cannot save."

3. Human Nature:
The Sinful Human Being

> The web of our life is of a mingled yarn,
> good and ill together. Our virtues would be proud, if
> our faults whipped them not; and our crimes would
> despair, if they were not cherished by our virtues.
> Shakespeare, *All's Well That Ends Well*

In *Perelandra* C. S. Lewis depicts a newly created and still unfallen world—but a world subject to temptation.[1] It is a world mostly of floating islands, though it also has a Fixed Land. The Lady in the story, an Eve figure, is constrained by certain commands of Maleldil, her creator. In particular, she (and the King, an Adam figure) are permitted to go onto the Fixed Land but forbidden to live or sleep there. The UnMan, source of temptation in Perelandra, uses this fact to unsettle the Lady; for, when she misses the King, who is elsewhere, he notes that people who live on a fixed land cannot so easily be separated. They are not constantly thrown into the wave, and they can to some extent control their own destinies. The command to live only on the floating islands stands, he says to the Lady, "between you and all settled life, all command of your days."[2] And this is true, though in a deeper sense than the Lady first understands. When temptation has finally been overcome, she sees the meaning of Maleldil's command.

58

The reason for not yet living on the Fixed Land is now so plain. How could I wish to live there except because it was Fixed? And why should I desire the Fixed except to make sure—to be able one day to command where I should be the next and what should happen to me? It was to reject the wave—to draw my hands out of Maleldil's, to say to Him, "Not thus, but thus"—to put in our own power what times should roll toward us . . . as if you gathered fruits together to-day for tomorrow's eating instead of taking what came. That would have been cold love and feeble trust. And out of it how could we ever have climbed back into love and trust again?[3]

Floating islands and Fixed Land—to be content with the former is to live by faith, to crave the latter is to grasp for a security of our own fashioning. This is the truth about and the test of human existence—and, unlike the Lady on Perelandra, we have failed the test. Created for life with God, humankind has failed in trust. And having rejected the wave, we cannot of our own power climb back again into love and trust.

I. Sin as Pride and Sloth

Our sin is best characterized as failure to master the intricate simultaneities required by the duality of our being. Created as embodied person and personalized body, located within the world of nature and history but made also for the eternal God, we ought to affirm the world as a reflection of God's goodness, but a reflection to be loved in God and offered back to him. The meaning of sin is that the two aspects of our nature quarrel, and we fail to make this double movement properly. In pride we seek only to be free; in sloth we want only the security of finitude and its limits.

We may refuse to accept the natural limits of our creaturely condition. That failure of trust is pride, and within Christian thought it has signified a failing more fundamental than mere vanity. It is the attempt to exercise freedom without limit — without, even, the limit that is God. In pride we pretend that the limits of our nature are of no consequence — that the inner meaning of history is simply the process of human self-determination. We think of ourselves as persons using their bodies and world, not as embodied persons. We hypothesize that freedom to transcend natural limits and determine our being is the final truth about human nature. Dominion over the co-creation becomes technological mastery. Augustine's description of Satan's sin is the classical description of pride: "he refused to be subject to his creator, and in his arrogance supposed that he wielded power as his own private possession and rejoiced in that power."[4] And Augustine goes on at once to add: "He has refused to accept reality." When we try to live as if we were not dependent beings, we make war on the truth of the universe, and — however giddy the sensation — we must ultimately fail to flourish.

We may also, however, fear the dizzy heights of the historical freedom that is rightly ours. Such failure of hope the tradition has called sloth. And as pride is a sin far more pernicious than vanity, so also sloth is something different from laziness. In his well-known essay on leisure, Josef Pieper makes clear how far we are today from understanding the evil that makes sloth a vice.[5] Captured by an ethos which exalts the place of work and finds in it life's significance, we can only regard sloth as that laziness which keeps us from work. Pieper notes, however, that one sign of sloth is the inability to enjoy leisure! Such an inability is closely related to another: inability to delight in the world. All genuine pleasures of life come from the hand of God, are shafts of his glory penetrating our experience, and are meant to lead us from creature to Creator.

> The heavens are telling the glory of God;
> and the firmament proclaims his handiwork.

Day to day pours forth speech,
    and night to night declares knowledge.
There is no speech, nor are there words;
    their voice is not heard;
yet their voice goes out through all the earth,
    and their words to the end of the world.

(Psalm 19:1-4)

We may refuse this movement from creature to Creator, refuse to acknowledge the heart's longing for God. But to stifle that restlessness is sloth. Fleeing the freedom that would take us beyond nature and history to the One for whom we are made, we simply try to hang on to what is given. But earthly goods cannot bear the whole weight of the heart's longing, and sloth ends in boredom and loss, even, of desire.

The end of both pride and sloth is the solitude that is hell. In pride we seek to make everything and everyone else subject to our will—a world in which the swollen ego is secure because alone. In sloth the self is equally alone, unable to delight in anything outside itself. "The solitary self to which pride is devoted in its final stages is at one and the same time the bored self."[6]

But that is the end of the road—when pride trusts nothing outside the self and sloth hopes for nothing beyond the self. When in sin our finitude and our freedom quarrel, one of these must be our destination. Since they are ultimately the same destination—isolation within oneself—it makes little difference which path we take. Yet, it may make at least some difference to those around us. There is one sense in which pride is a sin more fundamental than sloth: its consequences for others may be worse. Just as the Stoic is a harsher figure than the Epicurean and less likely to be simply an agreeable companion, even so the proud man may create more friction in life than the slothful man. Sloth is, at least initially, a more social vice. It does not deny our need for companionship with others, even if it lacks the courage to desire The Other. By contrast,

> pride is *essentially* competitive—is competitive by its very nature—while the other vices are competitive only, so to speak, by accident. Pride gets no pleasure out of having something, only out of having more of it than the next man.... Greed may drive men into competition if there is not enough to go round; but the proud man, even when he has got more than he can possibly want, will try to get still more just to assert his power.[7]

And because pride is essentially competitive in this way, because at its very root it sets us against the good of others, its effect on human life may be more immediately destructive than sloth.

Short of hell itself, neither pride nor sloth can attain its full development in a human being. We fail in trust— but not so fully that we cannot sometimes recognize our limits and our dependence. We fail in hope—but not so fully that we do not sometimes experience the longing of the restless heart. Because our faith and our hope are thus divided, our love must be as well. Our love for our fellow human beings and for the co-creation always flirts with idolatry. That the vice of sloth, clinging desperately to any good which promises to satisfy, should create idols is perhaps obvious enough. But pride is also a powerful maker of idols. St. Augustine, for whom the sin of Adam was preeminently pride, offers an illustration of the way in which pride may create an idol and thereby seem even altruistic. Eve was deceived by the serpent, but, Augustine writes,

> we cannot believe that the man was led astray to transgress God's law because he believed that the woman spoke the truth, but that he fell in with her suggestions because they were so closely bound in partnership.... Eve accepted the serpent's statement as the truth, while Adam refused to be separated from his only companion, even if it involved sharing her sin.[8]

We will miss the nobility and lure of pride if we do not see what Augustine here discerns. Adam preferred a union in sin to separation from his companion. The devotion and grandeur of such commitment are not without their appeal. That this devotion is founded in a pride which wants to order its own world rather than let it be ordered by God and which must one day lead, if uncorrected, to the solitude of hell, does not diminish the fact of love and commitment here displayed. If this is vice, it is "splendid vice." If it is *disordered* love, it is nonetheless disordered *love*.

The sinful human being is, therefore, whether in sloth or in pride, a maker of idols. In sloth we cling to the created good, hoping for a satisfaction which can in truth be found only in God. In pride we seek the solitary honor of creating and determining value; we make idols because reality intrudes and we find it difficult to trust only ourselves and live for ourselves alone. To say that we are sinners does not, then, mean that we love nothing outside ourselves, nor does it mean that we fail entirely in love for God. It means that our loves are torn and divided — "a mingled yarn, good and ill together." The final destination of sin may be a solitude that is hostile not only to God but to everything other than the self, but here and now sin is far more ambiguous: genuine love for God, even a desire to rest in God and accept our dependence on him — but, at the same time, an implacable will not to be interfered with, a wish to live autonomously. Sincere longing for the joy that only God can offer — but, at the same time, a timorous clinging to the goods we know.

The sinful creature is precisely that: a *creature* made for God, who cannot entirely shake off the longing for that appointed destination or close his ears to the address for God; a *sinner* who rebels against any goal she has not set for herself or who draws back from the dangers of a journey beyond the familiar. And because the sinful creature is both, pride and sloth must be chiefly descriptions of our ultimate destination apart from grace. But within human history these two fundamental vices work out their consequences in disordered, ambiguous, idolatrous loves — loves sometimes so splendid that we may hesitate to call them vice, sometimes so perverse that they may seem to have reached journey's end and cast off all ambiguity. But most often, they are simply torn and divided. This is the condition of sinful creatures who, having failed to respond with trust and hope to the address of God, must live with their divided loves.

II. Original Sin

This quarrel within our nature is, we now note, a historical, not an ontological truth. That sin is a corruption of our nature rather than essential to it is expressed in the Christian teaching of the Fall into sin — into that state or condition termed 'original sin.' As many have noted, the point of this teaching is not really to explain the origin of sin. Indeed, its point must be precisely the opposite: to leave sin unexplained and inexplicable, a surd in the universe. That this is the right way to read the story of the Fall in Genesis 3 seems clear. The first evil will is not explained by the story — but presumed. The tempter is already there. And if we ask how this should be, the answer can only be that the evil will erupts without explanation.

But it does erupt, and it need not have; it is not built into human nature. This suggests that we should not speak of the Fall into sin as, in Reinhold Niebuhr's terms, "a symbol of an aspect of every historical moment in the life of men."[9] To think of it that way — as a symbolic representation of a nonhistorical truth — is, in effect, to understand sin ontologically rather than historically. Niebuhr does, in fact, assign the state of original perfection to a moment "outside of history."[10]

In a moment of self-transcendence — a moment of "perfection before the act" — the self "knows itself as merely a finite creature among many others and realizes that the undue claims which the anxious self in action makes, result in injustices to its fellows."[11] Thus, according to Niebuhr's account, sin is inherent in our finite condition, perfection can exist only apart from it in an eternal moment — and we have, in effect, not a quarrel between the two aspects of the self but an ontological division. Perhaps a better way to make sense of the story of the Fall — that human beings are now in a condition of sinfulness, that the origin of this condition can neither be explained nor attributed to our created, finite condition, and that this need not have happened — is to say that "if there are other rational species than man, existing in some part of the actual universe, then it is not necessary to suppose that they also have fallen."[12]

Although the idea of original sin must in many ways seem paradoxical or even dubious, it has as well a kind of sensibleness, and it may account better for our experience of evil than other, less paradoxical stories. Thus, for example, G. K. Chesterton suggested that a person somehow knows

> that the ultimate idea of a world is not bad or even neutral; staring at the sky or the grass or the truths of mathematics or even a new-laid egg, he has a vague feeling like the shadow of that saying of the great Christian philosopher, St. Thomas Aquinas, "Every existence, as such, is good." On the other hand, something also tells him that it is unmanly and debased and even diseased to minimise evil.... These vague but healthy feelings, if he followed them out, would result in the idea that evil is in some way an exception but an enormous exception; and ultimately that evil is an invasion or yet more truly a rebellion.... It is the prince of the world; but it is also a usurper.[13]

There is something to this. A story that expresses the inevitability of sin while still making it parasitic upon the good it corrupts does illumine much of our experience. But fundamentally, Christian understanding of our bondage to sin begins with Christ, who is confessed as the deliverer from that bondage. It is in order to speak rightly of him that we go on to tell our own story and that of humankind.

In Romans 5, the one extended biblical treatment of what we may call original sin, Paul's theme is essentially Christological. His point is that grace abounds in Christ. "For as by one man's disobedience many were made sinners, so by one man's obedience many will be made righteous. . . . Where sin increased, grace abounded all the more." Those who know the story of Jesus and have come to trust him will be assured of the Creator's good favor toward his creation, but they will be equally certain that the power of sin cannot be minimized.[14] Both are central in the story of Jesus. Had the grip of sin upon our nature been less powerful, there need have been no cross (as, in effect, Augustine argued against Pelagius). And yet, this cross displays not only the seriousness of sin but also the goodness of God who wills to share the sinner's fate. These are the realities of Christian existence; the story of creation and its corruption by sin is not to be told in any way that undercuts these truths.

We could tell a story in which the evil of our world was illusory, but then there would be no need for any work of redemption in Christ. We could darken that picture a bit and understand sin as an imperfection which could be overcome with the help of a good example, but then there need be no cross in the work of redemption. We could construct a narrative in which simply to be finite was to be trapped in a sinful condition, but then the good God who in Jesus shares our fate would be hard to identify with the creator, to whom we would be strangers. By contrast with these possible narratives, the story Christians have told has been intended to necessitate Christ: of a creation good in the sense that finite creatures need not have been alienated from God, then a fall from that goodness, a failure of trust and a disordering of love so deeply infecting our nature that it becomes a condition from which we cannot free ourselves; the human will now a "free will in bondage" that is no longer oriented toward the God we are created to trust; finally, redemption and deliverance through God's re-creating act in Christ. Hence, the Christian understanding of original sin is, first and foremost, a working out of the right way to tell the story of Jesus. And in this sense, at least, Augustine was surely correct: "Now, whoever maintains that human nature at any period required not the second Adam for its physician, because it was not corrupted in the first Adam, is convicted as an enemy to the grace of God. . . ."¹⁵

To be sure, this remains a bewildering notion, since the noun *sin* suggests a responsibility that the adjective *original* casts doubt upon. The more we emphasize that fallenness is a condition which precedes any personal decision or act on our part (fallenness as an orientation of the will away from trust in God), the more we may seem to equate fallenness with fatedness and thereby jeopardize its character as sin. If, seeking to avoid this danger, we depict fallenness simply in terms of a personal decision or act for which we are clearly responsible, our condition of sinfulness seems to have its origin in a decision freely made from neutral ground. By constructing such neutral ground to make place for responsibility, we lose the sense of enslavement to sin. Neither of these provides what is needed: a description of "a powerlessness that is simultaneously an unwillingness."¹⁶ We need a confession of bondage to sin that does not degenerate simply into a complaint about the situation in which we find ourselves.

Satisfactory theoretical expression of such a concept is difficult, but it may seem less paradoxical if we tell a story which might be the story of any one of us. Imagine what might happen if

> a very badly brought up boy is introduced into a decent family. They rightly remind themselves that it is "not his own fault" that he is a bully, a coward, a tale-bearer and a liar. But, however it came there, his present character is nonetheless detestable.... [T]hough the boy is most unfortunate in having been so brought up, you cannot quite call his character a "misfortune" *as if he were one thing and his character another.* It is he — he himself — who bullies and sneaks and likes doing it. And if he begins to mend he will inevitably feel shame and guilt at what he is just beginning to cease to be.[17]

This is just a short story, perhaps only the outline of a story, but it discloses something like "a powerlessness that is simultaneously an unwillingness." What an observer's theoretical standpoint cannot at first explain without paradox is displayed in the story in such a way that the reader can enter into the experience of a condition *in* which one simply finds oneself but *for* which one is nonetheless responsible. This suggests a sense in which original sin might be both original *and* sin — something more than original misfortune. It directs us to the right kind of theory. Many of the puzzles that bother us when we contemplate original sin may result from a misunderstanding of the human person. A person is, to be sure, an individual — but an individual whose character is shaped and formed by the human community. We may rebel against that fact. We may argue that we cannot be held responsible for deeds that flow from a character formed by others. But that is to pretend that we are one thing and our character another — as if the self were something other than the self shaped within society. Behind our tendency to transform a condition of original sin into original misfortune is a false individualism which depicts the self as complete and whole entirely apart from life *beside* fellow human beings.

To recapitulate: The story of Jesus leads us to speak of original sin. The paradoxes of such a concept direct our attention to its point within anyone's personal story. And that, in turn, now brings us to a point from which we can perhaps make sense of the story of Adam—of sinful humankind. St. Paul writes in Romans 5:12 that "sin came into the world through one man and death through sin, and so death spread to all men because all men sinned." These words, much fought over in the history of interpretation, can perhaps never be clarified exactly. Almost certainly they do not mean what Augustine, misled to some extent by the Latin, thought they said: that "in Adam" all sinned. Neither, however, can they convincingly be taken to mean only that Adam sinned and suffered the consequences—and that when others, who stand in essentially the same position as Adam, likewise sin, they too suffer the consequences. That such a Pelagian reading would be mistaken seems clear from v. 19 which thinks of humankind as a whole (first united in Adam, then in Christ): "For as by one man's disobedience many were made sinners, so by one man's obedience many will be made righteous." The anti-Pelagian position, which became orthodox Christian teaching, held that the sin of humankind is transmitted by propagation rather than imitation. This in turn meant that the character of a person is determined not by his or her free choices but by a given condition— the orientation of the person away from trust in God. All choices are finally in service of that sinful orientation of the self. No one, therefore, stands on neutral ground as our first human parents would have. If their sin is inexplicable, ours is not; on the contrary, it flows readily enough from a nature corrupted by sin.

We cannot, of course, tell the story of the Creation or Fall into sin of those first parents. We can say only that the first human society resulted not simply from attainment of particular capacities—e.g., for rational, self-conscious thought—but from the address of God.

That address called forth the heart's desire for God, suggested human love as a faint reflection of the being of God, and authorized humankind to exercise dominion over the co-creation. How they refused the call of God we cannot say, but such refusal must have disordered their loves. And within such a community of disordered loves, attitudes and emotions are inculcated and shaped. In such soil human character takes root and habitual behavior develops. The character transmitted is, inevitably, a sinful and disordered one.

Since a human being is not an isolated individual but is shaped by human culture, we can discern a sense in which it is true that original sin is transmitted not by imitation but by propagation.

> Our humanity itself is a cultural heritage; the talking animal is talked into talk by those who talk at him; and how if they talk crooked? His mind is not at first his own, but the echo of his elders. The echo turns into a voice, the painted portrait steps down from the frame, and each of us becomes himself. Yet by the time we are aware of our independence, we are what others have made us. We can never unweave the web to the very bottom, and weave it up again.[18]

The transmission of human sinfulness is social, not merely biological. It involves imitation, in the sense that character is developed through imitation of exemplars. But this imitation goes far deeper than we wish, in our Pelagian moments, to concede. Before we stand on any neutral ground, able to choose among exemplars or reject all in favor of our own ideals, our character has begun to be formed and the orientation of our will established. This does not mean, of course, that we love only ourselves or that we are incapable of acting rightly. It means simply that our loves are torn and divided — and that, probe as deeply as we may into the self, we will find only such division. We are not wholly and entire creatures who trust.

This is not simply our misfortune — as if we were one thing and our character another. It is our sin. A sin that we in turn hand on, and a sin that deepens its grip on us through the choices of our own wills, which are free yet bound to the selves we are. This was Augustine's point in his powerful analysis of the division within his own will. He loved God and longed to give himself without hesitation to God, but "I was held back not by fetters put on me by someone else, but by the iron bondage of my own will. . . . From a perverse will came lust, and slavery to lust became a habit, and the habit, being constantly yielded to, became a necessity."[19] What we are pleased to call our self is, in reality, a legion of past selves and choices — ours and those who have shaped our character (and choices of still others who shaped theirs). At the same time, set against the power of sinful habit is the never-ceasing call of God: his address that calls us to trust and hope in him, to love our fellows, and to be priests of the co-creation. If we cannot entirely close our ears to that call, neither can we answer it with an undivided heart. This is human experience, and since the battle is waged within our experience, it will take a power greater than our own to overcome the force of sinful habit.

If something like this is an accurate account of our sinful condition, we need not deny that guilt and punishment accompany it. In Augustine's teaching, guilt (*reatus*) accompanied fault (*vitium*). This will seem paradoxical only if we forget the story of the boy badly brought up — who, when his character had begun to change, could not but feel shame and guilt at what he had been. Or it will seem paradoxical if we think sequentially — of a fault for which one is guilty, for which one must then suffer punishment. But the "punishment" of our fallenness is simply that we fail to flourish as human beings, that we turn from the One for whom we are made and miss the goal of our existence. What we need is not philosophical discourse on the concept of guilt, but, rather, deliverance.

To such a conclusion any discussion of human sinfulness should lead: back to the story of Jesus, which story first disclosed how far-reaching was the wrong turning humanity had taken, how crooked was the talk with which we were talked into talk. From the story of Jesus . . . to our own story . . . to that of humankind . . . and back to that of Jesus. "Wretched man that I am! Who will deliver me from this body of death? Thanks be to God through Jesus Christ our Lord." (Rom. 7:24f.)

4. Human Nature: The Justified Sinner

Why, all the souls that were were forfeit once;
And He that might the vantage best have took
Found out the remedy.
                    Shakespeare, *Measure for Measure*

The words of Lazarus Spengler's hymn capture the essential movement of the Christian story:

All mankind fell in Adam's fall,
One common sin infects us all;
From sire to son the bane descends,
And over all the curse impends.

As by one man all mankind fell
And, born in sin, was doomed to hell,
So by one Man, who took our place,
We all received the gift of grace.[1]

The "gift of grace" is central to the story through which Christians understand human nature and is at the center of their vision of the moral life. Human beings, sinful human beings, are also justified sinners. But how best to understand this truth about the grace of God — and how best to relate it to the moral life — has been a matter for discussion and disagreement throughout Christian history.

73

I. Transformation and Declaration

"Forgiveness, as a form of love which is beyond good and evil, is bound to be offensive to pure moralists."[2] We cannot but sympathize a little with the elder brother who was offended when his father welcomed the returning prodigal with open arms. "These many years I have served you, and I never disobeyed your command." If that makes no difference, the moral life seems unimportant. And yet, the waiting father also seems right when he says that it is fitting "to make merry and be glad, for this your brother was dead, and he is alive; he was lost, and is found" (Luke 15:29, 32). To make the grace of God—the justification of sinners—central in Christian life is always to risk offending the moralist in each of us. But to fail to run this risk is more dangerous still; for then we might become pure moralists who stand unequivocally with the elder brother and lose all sense of the fittingness of the father's forgiveness.

There is within Christian thought a permanent tension between two ways of understanding the grace of God. We may—in order to do justice to the elder brother's concern for progress in the moral life—think of grace chiefly as the transforming power of God underlying and sustaining the believer in the long and arduous journey from sinner to saint. We may also—mindful of the risk one runs in siding with the elder brother—think of divine grace as declaration rather than transformation: the pardoning word of forgiveness and acceptance of the sinner. From this perspective the Christian life is not so much a journey toward holiness as it is a constant return to the justifying word of God. There will also be progress, but it is often hidden under the cross.[3]

For each of these conceptions the grace of God is necessary and central in the Christian life; each affirms that Christians live *sola gratia.* When, however, we emphasize grace as transforming power, our attention is directed to the need for and importance of sanctification. Life is a journey toward holiness, empowered by the Spirit of Christ. When we emphasize grace as announcement of acceptance, our attention is directed and constantly redirected to the promise that Christ's holiness is ours *sola fide*. Life is a constant struggle to trust that we are what we seem not to be: righteous in God's eyes. Neither emphasis is free of danger. If grace is primarily a word of pardon to which sinners constantly return, we leave ourselves little scope or opportunity to speak of growth in that grace or progress in Christian living. Any language which suggests continuity of the self becomes suspect; for this image suggests a continual shattering of the self and negation of its achievements. But, on the other hand, if grace is chiefly transformation of sinners' lives through the power of Christ, we may seem at times to make grace conditional. Thus, Anders Nygren noted how the moralist might rewrite Jesus' story of the prodigal son, telling of

a father whose son had wasted his substance with riotous living in a far country and then returned to his father destitute but with good intentions; but the father, who knew from experience what such good intentions are usually worth, met his son's entreaties with the stern reply, "My house is closed to you until by your own honest work you have earned a place for yourself and so made amends for the wrong you have done"; and the son went out into the world and turned over a new leaf, and when he afterwards returned to his father he thanked him for the unyielding severity that led to his recovery, unlike the foolish softness and weak indulgence of some other fathers, which would have let him continue in his prodigal ways....[4]

Is this a gracious father? We have to admit that he may be. What seem to be conditions for the son's return may with some justice be described in a different way.

They are not, one might say, conditions for regaining the father's favor; rather, they are a description of the sort of son who would really want it. Only a son who returned in his way would be sufficiently transformed really to love his father. Only then would he have become a person who cared for the father and not simply the father's goods. Yet, even if we grant all this, we cannot avoid noting that this way of speaking about grace—though it is indeed a way of speaking about *grace*—may seem to undermine the unconditional acceptance of the sinner.

Because neither understanding of grace is danger-free, Christian thinkers will always find it necessary to use both ways of speaking—to characterize grace as both pardon and power.[5] This is a point worth illustrating, and we can do so briefly by reference to St. Augustine, for whom grace was primarily a transforming and sanctifying power, and Luther, for whom grace was preeminently a pardoning word of God.

In the story Augustine tells in his *Confessions*, divine grace serves chiefly to strengthen the soul in its movement toward God. Although he had gained from the Platonists some sense of the goal of life, Augustine thought he needed more. "It is one thing to see from a mountaintop in the forests the land of peace in the distance . . . and it is another thing to hold to the way that leads there."[6] Powerless to love God with a whole heart because of the division within himself, Augustine needed a grace of which the Platonists knew nothing: the Word made flesh. Only in the Mediator, the God-man whose very presence was grace, did he find the way back and the power to overcome the division within himself.

But a careful reading of Augustine's story will show that he could not say only this. It becomes clear in fact, though Augustine does not use Luther's language, that the journey back to God must be made *sola fide*. For none of us can really know how we are doing or how much progress we have made. We are unable to render judgment upon our character as a whole because no moment is available in which the whole of our life is present to our sight. We need to see the self whole and entire, but (as finite beings) we get only a succession of moments. In book X of the *Confessions,* when Augustine recounts not his past but his present, he makes clear this inability to know the self fully. He discusses (in X, 29-43) the state of his soul and considers what his progress in righteousness has been. Taking his categories from 1 John 2:16, he considers the degree to which he is still tempted by the lust of the flesh, the lust of the eyes, and the pride of life. Under the lust of the flesh he discusses various pleasures of the bodily senses — sex, food and drink, lovely music, the beauty of cultural artifacts — and takes stock of his susceptibility to their blandishments. The lust of the eyes that concerns him is a seeing that takes place with the eye of the mind — the temptations of curiosity and the desire to know. Although he knows that he is often still tempted and overcome by the pleasures of idle curiosity — when he stops to watch the hounds chasing a hare or a lizard catching flies! — he also knows that, by the grace of God, he quickly rises after falling and continues the struggle to attain holiness.

It is the third category of temptation — the pride of life — that most disturbs Augustine. Considering it leads him to realize that he cannot fully analyze his own progress toward righteousness, cannot see how far along he is on the journey back to God. What concerns him here is the desire for praise. And we should notice how Augustine states his concern. "But tell me, Lord, . . . has this third kind of temptation disappeared from me, or can it ever entirely disappear in this life?"[7] How, he wonders, do I know, when I am praised by others whether I refer that praise back to God's gifts of delight in it as praise due my own achievements?

How do I know whether I could get along without such praise? In the case of some other goods I can, if necessary, put myself to the test. I can give up wealth or high position and thereby determine whether my happiness truly depends on them or whether I seek it in God alone. But, of course, others might praise me for giving up these goods! Shall I try to live a bad life, so that no one will praise me? That hardly seems right. There is, he concludes, no satisfactory way to test my need for praise. "It still tempts me even when I condemn it in myself; indeed it tempts me even in the very act of condemning it; often in our contempt of vainglory we are merely being all the more vainglorious. . . . [8] Augustine thinks—and hopes—that much of the time his desire for praise is rightly ordered within his love of God. "But whether this is really how I do feel I do not know. In this matter I know less of myself than of you."[9]

The life story of such a man must surely be a *confession*—a confession of its faithful and its faithless character to the God who alone can see it whole. And thus the importance of the refrain which becomes in book X a powerful crescendo in the hands of a master rhetorician worrying lest he love too much the praise of men: "Give what you command and command what you will." The transforming grace of God will give what God commands. Augustine the sinner will be transformed into a saint. But in its context this is largely an affirmation of faith—trust that God will do what no human eye can discern.

With this we may compare Luther's famous little treatise on "The Freedom of a Christian."[10] The outline of the treatise is given in the two propositions Luther states at the outset:

(1) A Christian is a perfectly free lord of all, subject to none.
(2) A Christian is a perfectly dutiful servant of all, subject to all.

A neat and simple outline—but, as it turns out, there is an additional element in the argument, not present in the outline. Having discussed the pardoning grace of God and extolled the freedom which it brings, Luther turns to his second proposition. We expect him to develop at once the way in which faith, trusting the forgiving word of God, hastens to spend itself in service of the neighbor. Indeed, that is what Luther should do if the outline of the treatise were to remain intact.

But he does not. Instead, he begins the second half of the treatise with a discussion which seems, at best, unnecessary to his argument and, at worst, antithetical to it—a discussion for which the simplicity of the outline in no way prepared us. In this life, Luther says, a person must learn to control himself; "he must indeed take care to discipline his body by fastings, watchings, labors, and other reasonable discipline and to subject it to the Spirit."[11] With "joyful zeal" he must attempt to get the sinful passions under control. He must, we could say, take stock in the way Augustine did in book X. In short, Luther is pointing to the transforming work of grace in the believer's life, to the importance of discipline and growth made possible by the gracious presence of Christ's spirit.

Instead of a leap to the neighbor's side by one who believes the pardoning word of God, we are given first this call to discipline the sinful self. To say all that he needed to say about the Christian life Luther had to break the simplicity of his outline. For he knew that just as the "inexperienced and perverse youth need to be restrained and trained," so also the Christian, though righteous through faith, is not yet wholly perfected.[12] Of course, to put it that way may seem to take back what he had said in the first half of the treatise, that "true faith in Christ is a treasure beyond comparison which brings with it complete salvation."[13] But Luther did not take it back; he simply affirmed both truths. Grace is a word of complete pardon, and grace is the power of God to transform the life of the believer. To be honest about the reality of the Christian life he had to say both.

Luther could not speak of grace only as declaration of pardon. Augustine could not think of it only as transforming power. Each theological approach emphasized one understanding of grace, but neither man could say all he needed to say with one image alone. This will always remain true within Christian ethics. Grace is fundamental for the life of believers, but that grace must be understood both as pardoning word and transforming power. Within human history no theory can unite these two in a tension-free harmony. The ability to know which image of grace is called for at any given moment is, in fact, what makes the theologian. To speak of transforming power—of ethics!—to the returning prodigal would be to identify ourselves with the elder brother instead of the waiting father. But we cannot and should not deny the importance of the elder brother's concern even if we suspect that the day may come when he too will need to hear an unconditional word of acceptance.

II. Gift and Task

The tension between these two ways of describing divine grace is often put in terms of a tension between gift and task, indicative and imperative. If we understand grace as transforming power, there will be obvious room for imperatives which direct us toward the needed transformations, but God may seem more a commander than a giver and lover. It may seem more obvious that he commands what he wills than that he gives what he commands. If, on the other hand, we understand grace as pardoning declaration, there may seem little need for moral exhortation. The mere presence of imperatives might seem a vote of "no confidence" in the present tense of the gift.[14] Yet, in the New Testament and especially in the Pauline writings, indicative and imperative stand side by side. "If we live by the Spirit, let us also walk by the Spirit" (Gal. 5:25). Both gift and task are affirmed, and the tension seems firmly in place.

If it is correct to conclude, as I did above, that Christians need to speak of grace in both ways, we may anticipate that any attempt to overcome this tension will make it difficult to say all that needs to be said about the grace of God. How this can happen we may illustrate by considering one way—influential in recent years—of trying to overcome the tension between gift and task. Its programmatic statement is simple: "God's *claim* ... [is] a constitutive part of God's *gift*."[15]

What this means can be sketched quite briefly. The event of grace is the death and resurrection of Christ. In that event is demonstrated God's sovereignty and lordship over sin and death (the powers of the present evil age). This event is, therefore, the righteousness of God, which is "God's dominion over the world, which is being revealed eschatologically in Christ."[16] The gospel is an announcement that believers have a new Lord: the risen Christ, not the powers of sin and death. Grace means, therefore, transfer from bondage to one power to bondage to a new Lord. Because it does, gift and task are two dimensions of the one gospel, clearly and necessarily related. One who has been justified "stands under the aegis and hegemony of a new Sovereign."[17] And that—the giving of a new commander-in-chief—*is* the gift. Thus, the tension between indicative and imperative is resolved when we understand that the indicative, the gift announced and given, is the gift of a sovereign commander.

What happens to grace when gift and task are related in this manner and the tension between them apparently overcome? Although understanding the task as inherent in the gift, this approach does not present grace as transformation. If anything, in fact, it comes closer to picturing grace as declaration. But the gracious declaration is not simply a word of acceptance; it is the announcement of a master under whose claim one stands. The gracious God does not hesitate to exercise his sovereign right of command—though, presumably, he does this redemptively rather than retributively. How this might be understood has been aptly characterized by Victor Furnish. He suggests that we think of a juvenile offender whom the court refrains from punishing but, instead, attempts to rehabilitate.

> On the one hand, the court's decision not to prosecute may be regarded as tantamount to a verdict of acquittal. On the other hand, the court is empowered to place the "acquitted offender" in the setting which can afford him the needed redemptive relationships—perhaps his own home, a foster family, a "training school," or some other. By this means the court does not just make a "declaration" concerning the delinquent (which, in effect, has been acquittal), but causes an actual change in his situation. The court does not ignore the delinquent's disorientation and estrangement from society, but moves to overcome it. His acquittal does not involve a legal fiction, but presupposes that the new relationship which is being established can be reconciling and redemptive.[18]

But must we not now place "gift" within quotation marks? The "gift" is to be handed over to the benevolent tyranny of a reform school to have one's character worked on indefinitely. It is not the sort of gift one would describe as unconditional acceptance. Nor is it the sort of gift most likely to lead the juvenile to say of the court what St. Paul says of the believer in relation to God: "Since we are justified by faith, we have peace with God" (Rom. 5:1).

I do not wish to make the point more strongly than I ought. Like the prodigal in Nygren's retold parable, this juvenile might one day feel gratitude for the court's action. Thirty years later, when he is older, more mature, and wiser, he might look back on the course of his life and say: "That court showed me great favor when it placed me in the reform school; in fact, the change in my situation proved to be the gift of an entirely new life." But what can retrospectively be seen as gift cannot necessarily be experienced as gift in the present. It cannot be unambiguously experienced as acceptance.

What should we conclude, then, of the attempt to overcome the tension between grace as transformation and as declaration by understanding the task of the moral life as a constituent of God's grace? That it suggests a gift which is radically ambiguous. There is nothing logically inconsistent about it—just as no logical flaw is committed when the parent tells the child that she is being punished "for her own good." But not without reason has that parental statement become something of a joke. For children are unlikely to experience punishment and discipline as parental benevolence. A gift of that sort is not radical enough really to make peace.

The grace of God is pure, unconditional gift—acceptance, forgiveness, pardon. The grace of God is also the transforming power of his Spirit—committed to renewing and empowering those he has pardoned. From the perspective of the goal toward which God works, gift and task are indeed one. Not one in the sense that the gift is the announcement of a new taskmaster, but in the way Barth suggests: that embedded in the imperative is the divine promise to transform that imperative into a future indicative.[19] "You shall" is not only a requirement; it is a promise. God *will* give what he commands, not by placing the believer into a new situation of benevolent reform, but by the enabling power of the Spirit. But grace is also pardon. The unity of gift and task cannot often be experienced by one who stands short of the goal and who can trust nothing less than an unconditional acceptance.

"The issue at stake here," Reinhold Niebuhr wrote, "is whether man's historical existence is such that he can ever, by any discipline of reason or by any merit of grace, confront a divine judgment upon his life with an easy conscience."[20] Because we cannot, grace must be not only power but also pardon. This twofold view of the gift is clearly articulated in the third chapter of Philippians. There St. Paul expresses both the acceptance which the righteousness of God brings and the sense of imperfection which calls for progress in the Christian life.

> I count everything as loss because of the surpassing worth of knowing Christ Jesus my Lord. For his sake I have suffered the loss of all things, and count them as refuse, in order that I may gain Christ and be found in him, not having a righteousness of my own, based on law, but that which is through faith in Christ, the righteousness from God that depends on faith.... Not that I have already obtained this or am already perfect; but I press on to make it my own, because Christ Jesus has made me his own. (Phil. 3:8-9,12)

In short, gift and task must find their unity in God's will and work. The gift of God's good favor does imply — for Him — the task of bringing the sinner to perfection. For believers, however, there can be no easy resolution of the tension. Assertion of the task will often seem to deny the reality of the gift; it will, instead, awaken a sense of need for an ever-renewed appropriation of the gift. And similarly, the gift, when really experienced as gift, will seem to require no imperative as a spur toward action. There is no way to overcome this tension within our life. The *agape* of God poured into the believer's heart through the Holy Spirit brings peace with God *and* empowers the new life in Christ.[21]

III. The Love That Flows from Trust

To be pardoned by God is to be able to trust God to care for us. If the Father vindicated his Son by raising him from the dead, he can be relied upon to care for those who are his. Christian love can, therefore, afford to be free from concern for self. This does not mean that we give up our own projects and purposes in the world — a misconception treated above in chapter two. Self-reference should not be equated with self-love. But neither can the moral life be governed by any theory which suggests that we must treat the self in the same way we treat others. However plausible such a claim may seem (since if all human beings are to be treated equally, there would seem to be no more warrant for *under*valuing the claims of self than for *over*valuing them) it is not the wellspring of Christian love. Particularly in contexts where a use of force seems necessary, many Christians have believed that it was right to do for the sake of others what they ought not do in their own behalf.[22]

Hence, the life of love diverges from a philosophical principle of equal treatment of human beings. It diverges not because Christians love their life less than that of any other person, but because they have entrusted that life to God. It is in safekeeping. Of course, God may well care for us by moving others to use force on our behalf. And God may, in turn, care for them by moving us to use force in their behalf, even though we ought not use it for ourselves. Peculiar as this may seem to the outsider, it is not to those who have been grasped by that Emperor whose courtesy decrees that no one may paddle his own canoe and everyone may paddle his fellow's. The Christian life of love is governed not by a theory about equal treatment but by faith which trusts God and is, then, living and active in service of others. Some Christians hold that the use of force is always forbidden those who trust God, and theirs is certainly an authentic discipleship. Better, however, is an understanding that permits neighbor-love to flow from trust by distinguishing what we do for self and for others.

To understand love in this way enables us to come to terms with the "hard sayings" of Jesus in the Sermon on the Mount—and to do so in a way that neither loses their force nor turns them into a prescription for governance of the world or withdrawal from the world. "You have heard that it was said, 'An eye for an eye and a tooth for a tooth.' But I say to you, Do not resist one who is evil. But if any one strikes you on the right cheek, turn to him the other also. . . . " (Matt. 5:38-39). Luther captures in one sentence the meaning of such love: "Although you do not need to have your enemy punished, your afflicted neighbor does."[23] That is, God may use us as the means of protecting a neighbor's well-being, making us thereby the means by which that neighbor's trust in God is vindicated. But God would not have us defend *our own* well-being; instead we are to wait in trust for him to defend us—which he may, of course, do through a neighbor who protects our rights and meets our needs. This is the love Jesus tells his followers to enact. That he directs these words to his disciples is important. This love, so heedless of self, is not a natural possibility by which the world may be governed, nor, even, is it best thought of as something Christians should *require* of one another. Rather, it is a love that becomes a new possibility in the lives of those who have experienced grace as transforming power. All believers are only on the way toward such Christlike love, and a trust strong enough to eschew attempts at self-vindication is better thought of as new possibility than new law.

> In the one case, you consider yourself and what is yours; in the other, you consider your neighbor and what is his. In what concerns you and yours, you govern yourself by

the gospel and suffer injustice toward yourself as a true Christian; in what concerns the person or property of others, you govern yourself according to love and tolerate no injustice toward your neighbor.[24]

Thus we are enabled both to enact our trust in God to care for us (and to suffer, still trusting, when he seems not to care) *and* to heed his call to be the means by which he cares for others in need. We do for them what we ought not do for ourselves; this is the shape love takes when it flows from trust.

It is even possible that faith — and the love that flows from it — may be compatible with action which appears purely self-serving. Luther formulates the issue in this way:

> You may ask, "Why may I not use the sword for myself and for my own cause, so long as it is my intention not to seek my own advantage, but to punish evil?" Answer: such a miracle is not impossible, but very rare and hazardous.[25]

Luther then offers the example of Samson, who repaid the Philistines for giving his wife to another man by setting loose in their fields and orchards three hundred burning foxes as a kind of living torch. When questioned about his action, Samson responds, "As they did to me, so have I done to them" (Judg. 15:11). But, Luther suggests, Samson was acting not in his own behalf but in an official capacity!

> Samson was called of God to harass the Philistines and deliver the children of Israel. Although he used them as an occasion to further his own cause, still he did not do so in order to avenge himself or to seek his own interests, but to serve others and to punish the Philistines. . . . No one but a true Christian, filled with the Spirit, will follow his example. Where reason too tries to do likewise, it will probably contend that it is not trying to seek its own, but this will be basically untrue, for it cannot be done without grace. Therefore first become like Samson, and then you can also do as Samson did.[26]

If Luther's reading of Samson's motives is not altogether convincing, the principle he articulates is thereby only made more certain. Such a miracle — of seeming self-service which is really service to a neighbor — "is not impossible, but very rare and hazardous." It could happen only if the agent was entirely unconcerned with the fact that his own good was also at stake, only if all that mattered to him was that the good of a human being was here in need of vindication. If that is what it would take to be like Samson, we may rightly hesitate long before we seek to do as he did.

But what we hesitate to do in our own behalf — what Jesus enjoins his followers not to do for themselves — we may rightly do for the sake of others who are in need and to whom we have been given as caretakers. Only thus is love permitted to flow from trust and not placed entirely in opposition to trust.

5. Moral Theory:
Rules, Virtues, Results

Desdemona. Wouldst thou do such a deed for all the world?
Emilia. Why, would not thou?
Desdemona. No, by this heavenly light!
Emilia. Nor I neither by this heavenly light.
I might do't as well i' the dark.
Desdemona. Wouldst thou do such a deed for all the world?
Emilia. The world's a huge thing; it is a great price for a small vice.
Desdemona. In troth, I think thou wouldst not.
Emilia. In troth, I think I should; and undo't when I had done. Marry, I would not do such a thing for a joint-ring, nor for measures of lawn, nor for gowns, petticoats, nor caps, nor any petty exhibition, but for all the whole world? Why, who would not make her husband a cuckold for all the whole world? I should venture purgatory for't.
Desdemona. Beshrew me if I would do such a wrong for the whole world.
Emilia. Why, the wrong is but a wrong i' the world; and having the world for your labor, 'tis a wrong in your own world, and you might quickly make it right.
Desdemona. I do not think there is any such woman.

Shakespeare, *Othello*

The fundamental temptation, especially for those who are serious about the moral life and who may be

89

willing to seek the good of others in ways they would
not seek their own, is always the same: failing in trust,
our temptation is to love without limit, wanting to be
like God. "What the serpent has in mind," Karl Barth
has written, "is the establishment of ethics."[1] This is
an overstatement, but it points to an important truth.

I. Theories of Morality

The number of possible moral theories is not large,
though their varieties are infinitely complex. C. S. Lewis has a homely illustration which directs attention to
the features of life that any moral theory must consider.

> Think of us as a fleet of ships sailing in formation. The
> voyage will be a success only, in the first place, if the
> ships do not collide and get in one another's way; and,
> secondly, if each ship is seaworthy and has her engines
> in good order. As a matter of fact, you cannot have either
> of these two things without the other. If the ships keep
> on having collisions they will not remain seaworthy very
> long. On the other hand, if their steering gears are out
> of order they will not be able to avoid collisions. . . . But
> there is one thing we have not yet taken into account. We
> have not asked where the fleet is trying to get to. . . . And
> however well the fleet sailed, its voyage would be a failure
> if it were meant to reach New York and actually arrived
> at Calcutta.[2]

The analogy suggests three considerations that are important in morality:

(1) We judge *actions* as *right* or *wrong* (just as we
know that ships must not collide and get in each
other's way), and we may think of human beings
as having a right not to be wronged in certain
ways.

(2) We judge *character*, evaluating not just the right-
ness or wrongness of actions but also the *goodness* or *badness* of *agents* (just as we know that

the engines and steering gears of the ship must be in good order).

(3) We evaluate the *results* of action, the *goals* at which action aims and the *values* it seeks to realize (just as it makes a difference what the ship's destination is).

Any ethical theory will, in fact, try to take account of all three features of the moral life; yet, the distinctive shape of an ethic will depend largely on which of the three it makes central. Because this is true, it has become commonplace to distinguish three different kinds of moral theories. A *consequentialist* ethic makes the results or consequences of action central in moral deliberation. A *perfectionist* ethic emphasizes the character of the agent, the way in which our actions both shape and flow from the person we are, both develop and enact character.[3] A *deontological* ethic evaluates action more than character but emphasizes the shape of the act itself: not what *happens* (as consequentialists emphasize) but what the agent *does*.

For a consequentialist theory the moral agent is essentially a kind of public person whose responsibility it is to evaluate from an impersonal standpoint the worth of possible states of affairs and, then, to seek the best overall outcome available. What the agent does is not what counts most morally. What counts is that he is in service of the best state of affairs possible. Perhaps the most illuminating way to describe consequentialism is this: It holds that an *ought to do* follows from an *ought to be*. If it ought to be the case that no one suffer horribly while dying, I (and we) ought to do what is necessary to minimize such suffering, even if on some occasions that means aiming to kill in an act of euthanasia. By contrast, a deontological theory makes it possible (though not necessary) to hold that I ought not to euthanize the suffering person even if doing so would result in the best state of affairs on the whole. The difference between the two views can be put this way: If I were to do this, "*things* would be better, what *happened* would be better.... But I would have *done* something worse."[4]

This suggests that the important distinction between consequentialist and deontological theories involves the kind of responsibility ascribed to the moral agent and involves, therefore, the character of the agent. Does the agent adopt a universal (and therefore impersonal) standpoint, regarding his own life as would an observer and feeling obligated to achieve all the good he can? Or does the agent seek to act in a particular way and be a person of a certain sort, not ignoring the consequences but also not believing herself fully responsible for achieving the best possible outcome? This way of putting the matter suggests that our threefold division of moral theories needs to be revised. The crucial classification is twofold.

There are some ethical theories—deontological or perfectionist in character—which do not ask the moral agent to step out of his location in nature and history or to be more than a human being bearing a real but limited responsibility for overall outcomes. These theories accept the moral importance of the agent's perspective—the importance of what he is and does, not just of what he brings about. To be sure, such theories, if they are to be adequate to our experience, can never ignore the results of action. Nor can they permit us to make moral judgments which represent only our personal perspective. The virtue of justice and the requirement that we act justly, for example, are both grounded in an understanding of the person not only as finite but also as free—free to transcend at least to some extent our limited, partial perspective in order to be fair to others. The freedom by which human nature is enabled to transcend its particular location means that we can and must consider what is required of us from the perspective of God, before whom all human beings are equal and in whom all are united.

But we are not free to try to be like God. Some moral theories seem to seek a standpoint more divine than human. Such theories—chiefly consequentialist, but also and interestingly, Kantian—in their search for an objective and impersonal perspective ask us to make moral judgments about the world from a position nowhere within that world. They ask us to will universally or accept responsibility for trying to produce the best overall outcome. Theologically, we may say that such theories are rooted in our prideful attempt to free ourselves from a finite location within nature and history.

It is perhaps no accident that one of the most powerful and influential ethical theories of the modern period—Kant's—has taught us to will as moral maxims only those which could be adopted as universal law. It has encouraged us to think that our glory lies in being free and autonomous, obeying no law except that which we legislate for ourselves in accordance with the universal requirements of reason—has encouraged us, in short, to develop a moral theory for beings who are all freedom and no finitude. Not without reason did Iris Murdoch write that "Kant's man had already received a glorious incarnation nearly a century earlier in the work of Milton: his proper name is Lucifer."[5]

That the twofold classification of moral theories suggested above really does illuminate something important can be seen in the ease with which some have managed to transform a Kantian ethic—usually described as deontological—into a consequentialist ethic. R. M. Hare's "universal prescriptivism" offers a contemporary version of a Kantian ethic. In making a moral decision, Hare contends, we are seeking a judgment which we would be willing to prescribe universally—willing to regard as binding upon any person in similar circumstances. (Hare terms this the "archangel" level of moral thinking, and we ought to recall that angels are not restrained by the limits of finitude that bind human beings.) How do we know whether we would be willing to make such a judgment in all similar situations? By seeking imaginatively to occupy, in turn, the positions of all others who are involved in the situation—seeking to determine whether we would be willing to occupy their position on another occasion. In this way we discover what is "best, all in all, for all the parties." And, Hare notes, "we see here how the utilitarians and Kant get synthesized."[6] But perhaps this idea of taking into oneself the desires and sufferings of the world, feeling even if only imaginatively all its pains and pleasures as equally close to oneself—this move which enables Hare to transform the formal Kantian urge to will universally into the material consequentialist search for the best overall outcome—is a project that should give even an archangel pause. Unless, that is, he prefers to reign in hell than serve in heaven.

This project—which enacts a certain kind of character—is best exemplified and most fruitfully examined in consequentialist theory, and to it we now turn. Utilitarianism was the first great example of such a theory. Classical utilitarians sought to rank possible outcomes according to the amount of pleasure or satisfaction which they offered the people involved, and they required moral agents to seek to produce the best overall (or, least bad) state of affairs. If we abandon the utilitarian notion that good outcomes can be described solely in terms of pleasure or satisfaction, we will speak more generally of maximizing good consequences (however characterized). 'Consequentialism' is therefore a wider label and more general description of this sort of theory than is 'utilitarianism'. Why might one be attracted to such a theory?

II. The Lure of Consequentialism

The power of consequentialist moral theory comes in large part from the fact that "it is the major recognized normative theory incorporating the deeply plausible-sounding feature that one may always do what would lead to the best available outcome overall."[7] This philosopher's formula has the kind of other-regarding ring which Christians are accustomed to praise, and we may be tempted to believe that there must be little difference between an act which maximizes good consequences and an act that is most loving. Indeed, the power of consequentialist theory — at least within our culture — may in large part be a result of the fact that it sounds like a secularized version of the Christian love command. It is, I will suggest later, a quite natural theory for those who remain morally serious but who have lost or left behind the Christian framework that gave content and specification to the command of neighbor love.

As a way of seeing how attractive such language may be — how strongly it may tug on the hearts of those committed to self-giving love of neighbor — and in order to suggest also its most important problems, I begin with the straightforward and readily accessible philosophical language of an earlier day. The Englishman William Godwin, now largely forgotten but in his day (near the close of the eighteenth century) a well-known philosophical anarchist, developed what we may term a 'consequentialist theory' in his provocative *Enquiry Concerning Political Justice.*[8]

Godwin explains that he will use the term 'justice' to signify all our moral duty, and he means this rigorously indeed. "If justice have any meaning, it is just that I should contribute everything in my power to the benefit of the whole" (p. 40). Or again, "it is just that I should do all the good in my power" (p. 45). So exacting a conception of our moral duty has its appeal, but it will immediately suggest two questions to the mind of any thoughtful person. How shall we reconcile this understanding of justice with our sense that we are obligated especially to those who stand in certain special relations to us, that we cannot regard them simply as parts of the whole we are to benefit? And, how shall we reconcile this conception of moral duty with our sense that we must see to our own needs and, even, our own pleasures, not simply think of ourselves as acting at all times in service of the general well-being? Godwin tackes each of these problems with characteristic rigor.

Suppose, he writes, a fire should break out in the palace of Fenelon, archbishop of Cambrai, while he is at work on his *Telemachus*. Suppose the fire endangers the life of Fenelon and of his chambermaid, but we can save only one. Because we are connected "in some sense with the whole family of mankind," it seems obvious to Godwin that "that life ought to be preferred which will be most conducive to the general good" (p. 41).

> Supposing the chambermaid had been my wife, my mother, or my benefactor. This would not alter the truth of the proposition. The life of Fenelon would still be more valuable than that of the chambermaid; and justice . . . would still have preferred that which was most valuable. . . .
> What magic is there in the pronoun "my" to overturn the decisions of everlasting truth? (p. 42)

Someone might object that gratitude should lead me to prefer my mother, were she the chambermaid, to Fenelon. After all, she has endured considerable pain on my behalf and had nourished my life when it was entirely dependent on her. Godwin admits that gratitude is owed for every voluntary kindness, but it is owed simply because such kindness is virtuous and deserves respect. The fact that a particular kindness was bestowed on *me* is of no moral significance. The act of kindness is equally meritorious "whether the benefit was conferred upon me or upon another" (p. 42). From one perspective this is, of course, perfectly true, but it would be puzzling indeed to suggest that someone else might owe gratitude to my benefactor for the kindness shown me. Godwin grants that, as things stand at present, our closest companions will often get the larger share of our gratitude; for we lack the ability to make the needed universal discriminations, and we will inevitably think those kindnesses we have experienced to have come from the most deserving benefactors. But this admitted fact "is founded only in the present imperfection of human nature" (p. 43).

What of the other problem? If moral duty requires "that I should contribute everything in my power to the benefit of the whole," where will time and energy be found for the personal undertakings that add delight to life — for good books and friends, enjoyment of sunrise and sunset, time spent in vocations which please but do relatively little to enhance the general good? This question Godwin takes up by asking about the "degree" to which we must seek the good of others. In particular, what sort of sacrifices on our own behalf may be required? "And here I say that it is just that I should do all the good in my power" (p. 45). Godwin grants, for example, a right to private property. But this is to be regarded entirely as a trust. "He has no right to dispose of a shilling of it at the will of his caprice. So far from being entitled to well-earned applause for having employed some scanty pittance in the service of philanthropy, he is in the eye of justice a delinquent if he withhold any portion from that service" (p. 46). Or again, with respect to our vocational choices, he writes: "I am bound to employ my talents, my understanding, my strength and my time for the production of the greatest quantity of general good. Such are the declarations of justice, so great is the extent of my duty" (p. 46). Here again, in order to eliminate the magic from the word 'my,' Godwin has eliminated something of great importance to human life — the possibility of undeserved generosity and a self-sacrifice that is praiseworthy because not obligatory. "It is therefore impossible for me to confer upon any man a favour, I can only do him a right" (p. 47).

There is much in Godwin's language that might appeal to one nurtured on Christian talk of love for the neighbor: The search for a perspective from which the seeming arbitrariness of personal preference will be eliminated; the readiness to bring our every thought and action under the rule of love; the sense that, since the neighbor may be anyone, the neighbor must be everyone and our task must be to maximize well-being—all these have been thought to be implications of Christian love. But we have already seen in an earlier chapter that a more patient image of love is needed— in which we affirm the peculiar moral weight of special bonds while thinking of them as bonds within which we are schooled in the meaning of love for any neighbor. To suppose that Christian *agape* should be equated with the impersonal attempt to maximize good consequences is to be deceived by a seductive but false imitation of love. We can begin to see this if we consider more fully the two problems we noted in Godwin's discussion. Both have to do, though in different ways, with the place of freedom in the Christian life. (1) Are there any limits on our freedom to seek what is best for others? *May* we always aim at the "greatest good" attainable? Or, are there limits on what should be done even in the best of causes? (2) Are we ever free from the obligation to measure our action by the standard of general well-being? *Must* we always aim at the "greatest good"? Or, are we to some degree free to pursue our own projects and desires, even if they do not serve the greatest good possible?

These are two quite different sorts of restrictions on our freedom. For philosophical ethics the first kind of restriction may seem more difficult to justify.[9] For Christian ethics, by contrast, in which self-giving is so central, the second kind of restriction may seem more problematic.

III. Freedom *from* the Pursuit of Good Consequences?

John Finnis has written of the "secret, often uncon-
scious legalism" of consequentialist moral theory: "its
assumption that there is a uniquely correct moral answer (or specifiable set of correct moral answers) to all
genuine moral problems."[10] Should Finnis be correct it
will follow that if we interpret the love command as a
command always to seek the best overall outcome, we
will destroy the freedom of the Christian life. One way
of putting this is to say that consequentialism demands
too much of us, leaves no room for personal autonomy.
It moralizes the whole of life — making every decision
a moment of obligation and requiring us always to seek
what is best overall. It is better, though, to say not
that consequentialism asks too much but that it asks
the wrong thing of us. It asks us to think of love apart
from trust — to imagine that the destiny of the world
lies not in God's hand but in ours. It interposes between
us and God a moral theory which destroys our freedom
to hear in *different* ways God's call to delight in the
creation and serve the neighbor's need. It makes us
public functionaries, servants of the general good, and
thereby destroys the goal of Christian existence as life
in God — a union in love of those who are different, who
hear the call of God addressed to them personally and
see the beauty of God with a vision peculiarly theirs.

An obligation to love separated from the freedom to
trust in God's providential care makes life a heavy burden indeed, for then we constantly bear the godlike
responsibility of providing in our every action for the
general well-being. The consequentialist must be a
stern moralist; each action must be weighed and cal-
culated to determine whether it really fosters the greatest good. To play with one's child, walk with one's love,
read a book, write a friend, work in a garden, devote
long hours to a work of art or craftsmanship, spend
one's talent in a small and narrow circle — all such pos-

sibilities given in the particular time and place that is
ours will (on this theory) require justification from the
impersonal standpoint of universal well-being. And
even if we think such justification possible, a task taken
up for that reason can never be the same. "The un-
bought grace of life" is missed when obligation replaces
freedom.

Pointing out that utilitarianism "seems to require a
more comprehensive and unceasing subordination of
self-interest to the common good" than rival moral theories, Henry Sidgwick called attention to a fact Mill
had noted: Although utilitarianism was sometimes crit-
icized as being base and vulgar (because it made max-
imization of pleasure central), the more plausible
charge was that it set too high a standard and de-
manded too much.[11] It is worth noting, once more, that
from a Christian perspective the point must be made
differently. For if love bears and endures all things,
any limit on our obligation to seek what is best on the
whole cannot finally be grounded in a supposed claim
to autonomy or personal independence. If there is such
a limit, it is grounded, rather, in the nature we have
been given: created by God to inhabit a particular location in nature and history. We are free to some extent
to transcend that location, required to some extent to
transcend it — but not to forget that ours is the freedom
of a finite, dependent body. To imagine that it is our
responsibility to adopt a more universal standpoint
than this is to want to be like God — and to fail in trust.

Indeed, when we forget this, the results for moral
theory are very peculiar. Sidgwick considers in some
detail a kind of practical perplexity confronting consequentialist theory. The theory enjoins us always to
act in such a way as to seek the greatest good overall.
But many pleasures — which would, presumably, contribute to a good outcome — can be experienced only if
we do not aim at them. Remembering Godwin, we may
use gratitude as our example. Perhaps what is best for

all is that each of us spontaneously express gratitude to our benefactors. Perhaps this will lead to a better outcome on the whole than if we distribute gratitude to those who are in fact the greatest benefactors of humanity. For if we do as Godwin recommends, we will lose the peculiar pleasure that comes (to both giver and recipient) from the experience of spontaneous and uncalculated gratitude. Godwin is prepared to argue this point: "Would not the most beneficial consequences result from a different plan; from my constantly and carefully enquiring into the deserts of all those with whom I am connected, and from their being sure, after a certain allowance for the fallibility of human judgment, of being treated by me exactly as they deserved? Who can tell what would be the effects of such a plan of conduct universally approved?"[12] Who can tell—but then, who would wish to make the experiment? Sidgwick certainly did not. Instead, he suggests that most of us, most of the time, ought not try to live each moment as if we were consequentialists. Most of the time we should be moved to act by ordinary human impulses rather than the desire to achieve what is best overall; for, he notes, "each person is for the most part, from limitations either of power or knowledge, not in a position to do much good to more than a very small number of persons; it therefore seems, on this ground alone, desirable that his chief benevolent impulses should be correspondingly limited."[13] Sidgwick here puts his finger on the important issue, but he misunderstands its significance—as if the problem were that the consequentialist merely sets too high a standard for human beings. It is as if we should give grudging acquiescence to our finitude while taking no real account of it in moral theory. What is needed, by contrast, is a glad affirmation of our finite nature and trust that we are free to be the sort of creatures God has made us.

Put most generally, the problem is that to aim in all one's action at producing the best overall outcome would almost surely make life worse; for it would — to mention only what is obvious — remove the great good of spontaneity from life. To deal with this problem, consequentialists inevitably find themselves suggesting that things will be better if people do not always aim directly at the greatest good — that is, if they do not always act as if they believed consequentialist theory! One result of this is to create division and incoherence within the self.[14] For we have adopted a moral theory that is very difficult to act upon. The reasons for action which the theory offers cannot take flesh in the motives which move us. Adopting momentarily an impartial perspective, we can use the theory to approve or disapprove our life, but we cannot really live it. We are divided within between the person who acts and the *persona* who theorizes.[15]

A more important result will be the creation of divisions not within but among selves — division between those who can rise to the impersonal standpoint of an objective calculator of general well-being and those for whom it is better to act without such reflection. And, of course, since those in the first group know that it will be better on the whole if those in the second group do not try to act as consequentialists, the theory takes on a highly manipulative cast. With better reason than he thinks Hare terms these two levels the 'archangels' and the 'proles'. A theory which calls upon the moralist to take responsibility for what is best overall creates division — both within us and among us. This should be no surprise, since this is what Christians believe the sin of pride always does.

Christian love does not, therefore, require that we seek in every moment to achieve what is best overall. It interposes no moral theory between us and the call of God and leaves us free to take up our callings with glad and trusting hearts. We love when we serve the neighbors whom our vocation places before us. Now, to be sure, this argument for limited responsibility is not an argument simply for "my station and its duties." We are finite; but we are also free, not limited entirely by our present location. Hence, Einar Billing has suggested that "the call constantly has to struggle against two adversaries: stereotyped workmanship and unresponsible idealism."[16] If the heart that trusts God does not seek unlimited responsibility for achieving what is best overall, neither can it be closed to the call for love and service in new ways. We might remember the famous exchange in Dickens's *Christmas Carol* between Scrooge and the two businessmen who are collecting for the poor. "Are there no prisons?" "And the union workhouses?" Scrooge's questions make clear that he is well satisfied with current provisions for the poor. The businessmen point out that, while prisons and workhouses continue to function, many people would rather die than go there.

> "If they would rather die," said Scrooge, "they had better do it, and decrease the surplus population. Besides — excuse me — I don't know that [they would rather die]."
> "But you might know it," observed the gentleman.
> "It's not my business," Scrooge returned. "It's enough for a man to understand his own business, and not to interfere with other people's. Mine occupies me constantly."[17]

Scrooge's vice is not that he fails to respond to this particular Christmas appeal; it is that he never responds to any neighbor whose need calls him beyond his business. Such decisions are always personal and particular. They cannot be made for anyone else. They cannot be willed universally for all similarly situated people. They cannot be made from an impersonal, objective standpoint that is nowhere in particular — for we never hear the call of God except at the place where we stand. In making such decisions in freedom we discover who we are and will be — and we are never solely servants of the general good.

IV. Freedom *for* the Pursuit of Good Consequences?

The argument of the previous section was that Christians *need not* always seek what is best overall. They are free from the tyranny of consequentialist theory. But another problem remains. Are there occasions when Christians not only may not but also *ought not* seek the best overall result in their action? Are there restrictions on our freedom to seek the good? This is the question posed especially by a deontological moral theory.

One could not ask for a more resounding answer than that furnished by Cardinal Newman, in a famous sentence couched in his intricate prose:

> The Catholic Church holds it better for the sun and moon to drop from heaven, for the earth to fail, and for all the many millions on it to die of starvation in extremest agony, as far as temporal affliction goes, than that one soul, I will not say, should be lost, but should commit one single venial sin, should tell one willful untruth, or should steal one poor farthing without excuse.[18]

Here indeed is a man who believes that an *ought to do* will not necessarily follow from an *ought to be*. It is quite clear that for Newman the focus of the moral life is on what we do and are, not what happens as a result of our doing.

Newman's statement is worth considering because, precisely by its very boldness and straightforwardness, it calls forth an obvious objection. How can we claim the name 'love' for the kind of action he describes? In *Silence*, Shusaku Endo's novel about Japanese Christians suffering persecution for their faith, the protagonist must make such a decision. A priest, he is asked to apostatize, to trample on an image of the face of Christ. If he does, the torture of his fellow believers will end. He will spare them that suffering and quite possibly keep them from themselves committing the mortal sin of apostasy. And when he finally does it, steps upon the face of Christ, he does so in the name of love. He believes, in fact, that the face of the bronze Christ urges him on, saying: "'Trample! Trample! I more than anyone know of the pain in your foot. Trample! It was to be trampled on by men that I was born into this world. It was to share men's pain that I carried my cross.'"[19]

What if, one may ask Newman, one "willful untruth" can prevent the "starvation in extremest agony" of millions? Or prevent many more such untruths from being told? Or stop the torture of one's fellow believers? Many may wonder whether such a price is not worth paying. And it may seem that any person genuinely moved by "love" could not refuse to dirty his hands by doing an evil deed whose results were so good. In a moment we will consider what Newman denies: that there might be circumstances in which one must do such an evil deed. But first we should understand why Newman is essentially right, how it is that he articulates a concern which must be central in Christian ethics.

From an impersonal standpoint our actions can perhaps be regarded as just a certain kind of event in the world, but as moral agents — as creatures made for communion in love with God, and creatures whose character is shaped in action — we can never so regard them. Our actions are not simply events in the world; they are occasions in which to come upon ourselves, to learn at least in part who we are.[20] They indicate whether we will trust God to care for us and the world he has made — or whether we have shouldered that burden ourselves. To aim at evil, even in a good cause, is to take into our person a choice against what is good — not just to let this happen, but to give it the personal involvement of our purpose.[21] It is to begin to make of ourselves people who would not want to be with God. This must be said in defense of Newman. This is why he is essentially correct.

But not entirely correct. It captures the truth of grace as power but misses the profound necessity of grace as pardon; hence, it fails to capture what is central in Christian ethics — a focus on the neighbor. The focus of one who trusts in God's pardoning grace must, especially in the exceptional moment, be not his own character but the neighbor's need; for, otherwise, his character cannot be fully shaped by the virtue of faith. The truly exceptional case will be rare, of course, and many such cases may be less problematic than they seemed at first and may suggest only the need for more complexity in the rules by which we govern our conduct. (Newman did not fail to see this. What he absolutely disavows, after all, is that anyone should steal a farthing *without excuse*.) But if and when we truly find ourselves in what Helmut Thielicke called the "borderline" situation, then we should say with Thielicke that "[l]ove is a capacity for improvisation directed to the moment."[22] We ought not, however, use such an exceptional moment as the basis for an entire ethic, as the occasion for construction of a moral theory by which to govern the whole of life.

Michael Walzer, writing of the morality of warfare, termed such exceptions instances of "supreme emergency."[23] The rules of war should not, he thought, ordinarily be broken even in a good cause, but the moment of supreme emergency is a situation in which they must be broken (though without denying that we incur guilt in doing so). An emergency is "supreme" when it is both *morally* and *strategically* necessary to break the moral rule for the sake of the desired outcome. Morally necessary — if it is imperative that we achieve our end, if failure here would mean not just the loss of certain goods but acquiescence to the rule of evil. Strategically necessary — because it must be true that no other way of resisting this evil is available to us. We cannot deny that there may be such a moment in which the sustaining presence of the God whom we trust is manifested in his seeming absence — an absence in which we are compelled to do what is needed to care for the creation.

Some will argue that to permit the possibility of an exception even in such circumstances must inevitably undermine the nonconsequentialist character of an ethic.[25] This might be true if the overriding of moral principle countenanced in the moment of supreme emergency were *justified* on consequentialist grounds. But Walzer offers no such justification; nor do I. Indeed his categories of moral and strategic necessity seek to describe the moment in which necessity truly has us in its grip — the moment when either we accept the rule of evil or, refusing to do that, invest evil with the involvement of our own purpose. A moment, in short, in which we are no longer free — except to cry out as St. Augustine's wise judge would: "Deliver me from my necessities."[25] The evil deed can still be done in such a moment as an act of trust, but only if this prayer is also uttered. It can be done not with a "good" conscience, but with a "comforted" conscience.[26] Thus, the moment of supreme emergency, like what Charles Fried has called the *catastrophic* as an ethical category, identifies a moment of necessity for which our usual categories of moral judgment are no longer sufficient.[27] Walzer's characterization of the moment of supreme emergency is, necessarily, general. And although some might wish that it should be made more precise, there is a good moral reason why it cannot be. In such circumstances the agent ought to face an internal struggle between the demands of morality and the hard chains of necessity. If moralists were able to specify justifying conditions in advance, this struggle — which is essentially the struggle to trust God — would not have to take place.[28]

Christians are called in every circumstance of life to trust God. This call delivers us from the tyranny which requires that we be something more than finite beings, that we always seek to produce what is (impersonally considered) the best overall outcome. But the call does more than free us from the pursuit of good consequences; it also limits the ways in which we may pursue them. We are not to seek the good by doing evil, by acting in ways that manifest our failure to trust God to care for us and the world, by seeking to take upon ourselves the burden of a divine providential governance. Hence, a Christian ethic need not and should not be consequentialist. And if a moment of supreme emergency should arise, a Christian can and will offer no justification for overriding the moral rules which bind us to our neighbors and thereby limit us. Christians must seek no impersonal standpoint from which to be justified in such a decision. If we are truly caught in the web of necessity, we must act. But if while acting we do not fail in trust, we will indeed — as Augustine saw — pray for deliverance and pardon from the God who is not bound by our necessities.

V. Is God a Consequentialist?

More than half a century before Godwin wrote his *Political Justice*, Joseph Butler, one of the greatest English moralists, argued that the moral obligation of human beings was not to produce the greatest good possible but to do good within the limits and restrictions placed upon us by moral law. Butler's reason for believing this was theological, and he did not attempt to understand human nature or our moral responsibilities in isolation from the Creator, upon whom our life depends. "The happiness of the world is the concern of Him who is the Lord and Proprietor of it; nor do we know what we are about when we endeavour to promote the good of mankind in any ways but those which he has directed, that is indeed in all ways not contrary to veracity and justice."[29] Human beings are not, Butler claimed, free to determine their responsibilities from a purely impersonal standpoint. They are always located in nature and history, and to be thus located is part of what it means to be human. Butler was willing to consider the "supposition" that God might be a consequentialist, but that would mean only that God had thought it best on the whole for us not to be [consequentialists] and had created us as beings whose freedom to seek the good was morally limited.

> The fact then appears to be, that we are constituted so as to condemn falsehood, unprovoked violence, injustice, and to approve of benevolence to some preferably to others abstracted from all consideration, which conduct is likely to produce an overbalance of happiness or misery; and therefore, were the Author of Nature to propose nothing to Himself as an end but the production of happiness, were His moral character merely that of benevolence; yet ours is not so. Upon that supposition indeed the only reason of His giving us the above mentioned approbation of benevolence to some persons rather than others, and disapprobation of falsehood, unprovoked violence and injustice, must be that He foresaw this constitution of our nature would produce more happiness than forming us with a temper of mere general benevolence. But still, since this is our constitution, falsehood, violence, injustice, must be vice in us, and benevolence to some preferably to others, virtue, abstracted from all consideration of the overbalance of evil or good which they may appear likely to produce.[30]

The movement from Butler to Godwin's position that "that life ought to be preferred which will be most conductive to the general good" represents in some ways the turn toward modern moral theory. And it is a movement *from* a conception of human beings as creatures always in relation to God and therefore always

limited in certain ways, *to* a quite different vision of
the human agent as the godlike bearer of an unlimited
responsibility for producing good results.

J. B. Schneewind has sketched the "story" of the rise
of modern moral philosophy in a way that suggests
such a theological point.[31] He notes that the moral philosophy of the seventeenth and eighteenth centuries
took place against the background of a received and
still deeply held—even if now also deeply challenged—
belief in the just and good providential governance of
God. The production of good at which the moral life
aimed was in no sense anyone's solo effort; rather, it
was a cooperative endeavor. All people were to carry
out the tasks given them and to respect the moral law
that tied their life together with others in various
bonds, and this could be done in the confidence that
they thereby played their part in an overall enterprise
whose final purposes were God's alone to determine.
"Thus," Schneewind writes, "no [human] agent has a
task properly described as producing the good." Since
human beings never fully understand the final goal and
the particular contributions different agents make to
it, they are never in a position to accept governance of
this entire cooperative undertaking—never in a position to take control of the course of history. "Hence,
for us our duties must always have an absolute deontic
status, although—as Butler points out—God may well
be utilitarian and may understand the laws of morality
in that sense."

But what happens if these religious beliefs begin to
fade? If for some people the whole of life, and not just
a moment of supreme emergency, seems marked by the
absence of God? It is not hard to see how it should be
that, for people who remain morally serious but who
lack the trust and hope in God that characterizes Christian life, consequentialism should seem a quite natural
moral theory. Just this is the plot of Schneewind's story.

Suppose the aim of the enterprise is human happiness, rather than cosmic displays of God's glory: then we can begin to understand the goal. Suppose God no longer intervenes in particular cases in the world: then we cannot be sure He will make up for failures by our fellows; then each of us has some degree of responsibility to see to it that the end is indeed brought about by doing our duty. The absolute deontic status is gone; we are required, morally, to judge to some extent by results. Thus, the inner logic of a cooperative venture carries us toward utilitarianism as an explanation.

If God is not available to produce the best overall outcome, and if it is important for human well-being that someone accept such responsibility, then human beings themselves are the most likely candidates. And so we succumb to the serpent's temptation in the name of responsible love.

At the same time, the old rules which govern the bonds of human cooperation will remain; they will exercise some claim over us even though we will not always be able to demonstrate that they serve to produce what is best overall. These rules may, therefore, come to seem rather puzzling and mysterious, since it will be hard for creatures who have accepted a godlike role to understand why they should accept any limits on their freedom to produce the good.

Thus, modern moral theory has tried to deal with the tension between the *good* and the *right* in quite a different way than did Butler, but we may wonder whether his way did not carry important Christian insight. This tension — between the worthwhile results we seek to produce in and for the lives of others, and the moral limits on how we are to act — is a permanent one in human history. If we try to eliminate it, we seek, in a sense, to save ourselves from it by means of moral theory. But for the heart that, trusting God, seeks to live through the tension, it is always occasion for temptation — a moment of danger in which, seeing that the

fruit of the tree is good for food, we will be tempted
to eat of it. It is temptation when the tension becomes
simply a call to daring and responsible exercise of freedom. But, in fact, this is no true human responsibility,
but only an illusion. "If, as consequentialism holds, we
were indeed equally morally responsible for an infinite
radiation of concentric circles originating from the center point of some action, then while it might look as if
we were enlarging the scope of human responsibility
and thus the significance of personality, the enlargement would be greater than we could support."[32] We
end, in short, with something that cannot be genuine
human responsibility.

The first article of the Christian creed characterizes
us as finite beings — limited and dependent, even if also
free to some indeterminate degree. The second article
of that creed affirms that the Father who has fixed the
bounds of our habitation has — to use the philosophers'
language for the moment — given his Son into death for
the general well-being. And if the first article of the
creed seems to restrict the means by which we may
pursue what is best, the second article seems to depict
a divine love which, if it serves as our example, might
make consequentialists of us all. Perhaps we discern
here a still deeper reason why the tension between the
right and the good cannot be eliminated from our world;
for it reflects not only our nature as finite and free,
but also God's action on our behalf in creation and
redemption.

We may doubt, though, whether Butler's "supposition" is anything more than an engaging thought experiment. The God of the Christian creed is not best
described as a consequentialist — as one who seeks what
is best by adopting an impersonal perspective from
which to manipulate our doings. Rather, that God is a
lover, who enters into our nature and history and never
fails to love those whom he meets here. If the Father
gives his Son into death, it is also true that the Son

willingly takes up this vocation and enacts it without failing in trust. This means that in his sovereign freedom God takes our finite being into himself, suffers its tensions, and overcomes them. For that reason we trust him; for that reason we do not seek to understand the meaning of neighbor-love apart from such trust; and for that reason we live in hope. It may be, in fact, that moral theory needs the hope that God can complete what remains incomplete in our limited strivings and can be trusted to work for good in everything. Without such hope we may be hard pressed to resist the lure of "results." But when the Christian virtues of trust, love, and hope mutually interpenetrate our character, we may recognize in consequentialist moral theory the voice of the serpent. And even if for most of us most of the time a theoretical mistake is not the greatest danger that lies in wait, it is still true that we are given here an opportunity to enact our trust in loving God, as we are commanded, with the mind.

6. Moral Knowledge:
The Limits of Redeemed Vision

Wisdom and goodness to the vile seem vile.
Shakespeare, *King Lear*

The Christian ethic that emerges from the argument of the previous chapter has both deontological and perfectionist features. There is place for rules — in particular, rules that set limits upon how we may seek the various goods that life offers. But rules do not tell the whole story, nor can commitment to them as a structured form of love be sustained apart from the virtues of faith and hope.

We can see this if we consider the seemingly simple commandments of the Decalog, to which Christians have returned for guidance in generation after generation. Taken as moral rules, each commandment will surely need to be made more complicated and complex; exception clauses and more precise characterizations may have to be added. In their context, however, they are also something more than rules; they are a brief picture of what it means to trust God in the whole of life. For the God who here commands identifies himself as the redeemer, the One who has delivered his people from bondage.[1] The commandments of the law's first table call for trust in this God; those of the second table specify how people who trust God to accomplish his

114

saving purposes ought to treat their neighbors. Luther's explanations of the commandments in his *Small Catechism* capture this essential connection by grounding all obligations in the God-relation: "We should fear and love God so that...."

Moreover, the commandments as Luther explicates them do two things: they set limits to our action, but they also demarcate a sphere of "the permitted." Thus, for example, Luther explains the commandment prohibiting murder: "We should fear and love God that we may not hurt nor harm our neighbor in his body, but help and befriend him in every bodily need." Some actions—which, of course, may need to be specified in rather precise detail—hurt and harm the neighbor. We should not seek to protect ourselves by those means, and, hence, our freedom is limited. But to respect those limits is not yet fully to enact this picture of trust. The limits—important though they are for human life and even if they were fully observed—do no more than mark out for us the immense expanse of life in which we are set free to serve others. If we are not free in the ways prohibited by the commandments, if those ways are not neighbor-love, then in what ways? In the countless ways which love finds but law cannot command. If God can be trusted to care for us, the energy that we might ourselves have devoted to that cause is set free for service to help and befriend the neighbor in every bodily need.

When faith is sustained by hope and active in love, it struggles to shape and inform the whole of life. Its powerful influence is set free in the worldly spheres in which we live and in which God orders our life—in family, work, and politics. God ordains marriage and sets the solitary in families; he establishes for humanity the task of tilling the ground and caring for the cocreation; he upholds the power of government to seek some measure of justice and peace. Through these worldly spheres God preserves human life, sees to our needs and those of our neighbors, and offers the hope for a fulfilling and flourishing life. But the God at work in these realms of life is the same God who in Jesus of Nazareth has delivered us from this present evil age and inaugurated the age which is to come.[2] Through the Spirit of the risen Christ, given to believers in baptism, God's love is poured into our hearts; yet, that Spirit is not only present gift but also ground of hope, the down payment on future redemption.[3] Hence, within this world Christians are to lead transformed lives, are to hand themselves over to the empowering and sanctifying grace of God; living in this age, in "the flesh," they live by faith in the Son of God, whose pardoning grace has made them his.[4]

Thus, Christians find themselves living in two realms, in this age and the coming age that is already also here—and both are God's. We live as children, parents, spouses, workers, citizens; yet, unless we wish to sever entirely the two realms of the one God's activity, we must affirm that it is faithfulness to which we are called in the worldly spheres of life and faithfulness in which they train us. The overarching rubric by which to interpret what is happening in spheres such as family, work, and politics is this: They are places where God, having set us free through his pardoning grace, sets before us others who need our care and faithful commitment. And they are schools of virtue in which, by God's empowering grace, our faith begins to learn the meaning of faithfulness. Hence, as Augustine said, the servants of God "have no reason to regret even this life of time, for in it they are schooled for eternity."[5]

Apart from such general statements, however, we should neither expect nor seek from Christian ethics any *single* principle by which to specify how Christian life must take shape within these worldly spheres. As justice may take quite different forms within different spheres of life, so too may faithfulness.[6] For example, the shape that faith active in and formed by love takes within a marriage may differ considerably from its political form. Moreover, an equality which is appropriate and desirable within the sphere of politics or work may be out of place within a bond like that of parent and child. We cannot simply apply a principle to all of life; instead, we must look to see what is called for in the different spheres in which we live. We may well ask, of course, how can one who is caught between the two ages of God's rule determine what is called for here and now? How can a vision not yet fully transformed discern the true meaning of faithfulness? What are the limits of our moral knowledge?

I. The Political Use of the Law

In chapter 1 I suggested that Christian ethics is fundamentally a singular ethic, shaped by the distinctive contours of the Christian story — but never solely that. When we consider how we might know the meaning of faithfulness in the different spheres of life, we should not forget that more general claim. This knowledge is in part the work of natural (i.e., created) reason, which, in Christian thought, has often been discussed in terms of a theory of natural law. By considering briefly the nature of such theories we can permit the perspective of chapter 1 to reassert itself. We will discover that we cannot adopt a natural law theory without being driven to raise certain theological questions, and they, in turn, may move us toward an ethic that makes use of natural reason without being grounded in it.

At the very least, a natural law ethic seeks to discern — on the basis of our God-given rational powers and apart from any special revelation — some standards of behavior or conditions of human association that apply to all human beings and societies (past, present, and future). We may develop such a theory from two rather different directions, however, and they give rise to quite different sorts of theories. One way begins by noting that the "natural" may refer to what we regularly observe in the world. That is, it may be essentially a descriptive category. Acorns grow into oaks. Only societies with the courage to defend themselves survive. In this sense what is natural is simply what we see happening regularly around us. To be sure, from this *de*scription we may seek to derive a *pre*scription (though always a hypothetical one): An acorn, if it is to fulfill its nature, ought to grow into an oak. Societies, if they wish to survive, ought to find ways to instill courage in their members.

Thinking of the natural in this way gives rise to an ethic that makes survival central and that describes the basic conditions necessary for any community to function effectively and survive. Natural law presents us with hypothetical imperatives prescribing the minimal requirements for social survival. Hobbes is often thought of as the father of such theories, and H. L. A. Hart's theory of "the minimum content of natural law" is a good example of such a theory in modern dress.[7] Hart invites us to consider certain givens about human beings and their world: We are vulnerable and easily harmed. We have relative equality in strength—and even the strong must sleep sometimes. We need things like food, clothes, and shelter—all of which may be limited resources. We need to find a way to make agreements with each other. From such facts, and presupposing our desire to survive, we might derive a set of minimal rules needed for human life in society—rules that would look rather like the second table of the Decalog: If we are to have some confidence in our association together, we will need to prohibit harming and killing. If the family is to function effectively as the basic unit of society, spouses will need to be able to trust each other, and parents will need to see that

the sacrifices they make on behalf of the next generation give rise to filial gratitude and esteem. If we are
to secure for ourselves some of those necessary but
limited resources, we will need institutional means of
protecting what belongs to one person or another. And
if agreements are to have any chance of lasting over
time, we must be able to trust the spoken word of
others. Putting the matter this way has the added ad-
vantage of allowing us to see the roots of such a theory
not only in Hobbes but also in the Reformation category
of the "political use of the law." When natural reason
discerns these imperatives, it is responding to God's
own urging and compelling action to govern human life.

We should not underestimate the difficulties of achieving even so limited an understanding of the meaning
of faithfulness in human communities. In the *Summa
Theologiae* St. Thomas writes that the first principles
of the natural law are self-evident.[8] This might be taken
to mean "obvious," as if any morality that is "natural"
must be obvious to the minds of all. But that is not
Thomas's meaning. He goes on at once to distinguish
two kinds of self-evidence. A proposition can be self-
evident *in itself*, he says, if it is what we call a tau-
tology—its predicate contained in the notion of its subject. And a proposition may be self-evident *in relation
to us* when we understand clearly the definition of the
subject and can see that the predicate is contained
within it. If we lack such understanding, the proposition—however self-evident in itself—will not be self-
evident in relation to us. Therefore, Thomas concludes,
some statements may be "self-evident only to the wise."
We may come only gradually to understand a truth
which, once seen, is self-evident (in the sense that it
shines by its own light and is derived from no other,
more fundamental truth).

When, therefore, we seek to understand how best to
structure our common life together, some development
in our moral knowledge is both likely and necessary.

St. Thomas himself thought that our passions and evil habits might often hide from us truth that ought to be evident to our natural reason. He offers an example: "Such was the case among the ancient Germans, who failed to recognize theft as contrary to justice, as Julius Caesar relates, even though it is an explicit violation of natural law."[9] E. A. Goerner has offered a helpful reading of this example, and I follow him here in explicating Thomas's point.[10]

It is unlikely that the Germanic tribes of whom Caesar wrote and to whom Thomas refers thought that all robbery was just. Their raiding and marauding was directed against those outside their own tribes (since, indeed, their society would be unlikely to have survived if they made no attempt to suppress robbery within their community). But these tribes, since they lived largely from plunder, could survive and even flourish while countenancing a good bit of robbery against outsiders. If such a policy would ultimately prove destructive, that consequence was hidden for a time by the effectiveness of Roman imperial power. Within the empire the long-term consequences of such activity could be controlled and hidden, and the tribes did not have to fear that their pattern of life might cause the collapse of the economic system upon which they depended. There was always more booty for the taking.

In time, however, the decay of imperial power meant that the raiding grew in proportion, and the seemingly endless supply of plunder was lost as the Roman economy began to collapse. What, then, did the Germanic tribes have to do? They were forced gradually to establish a political order that suppressed the constant robbing and raiding. Once the responsibility for a stable society became theirs, they themselves had to assert the requirement of the natural law against robbery. "In order to enjoy what was left of what they had taken from the Romans and in order to raise the defense forces necessary to protect it from the next wave of robbers, the Franks, for example, worked to set up a stable order of property that allowed the slow economic development of Gaul and parts of Germany. They had learned from nature itself the precept forbidding raiding."[11]

This is part of what it means to speak of a naturally known morality. If it is self-evident to the wise and good, still it is far from obvious. It can and must be learned, and that learning process may be a gradual and arduous one. Violate the meaning of faithfulness built into the created spheres of worldly life and you will eventually suffer. But the "you" who suffers may be no single, particular agent; any given violator may be one for whom vice pays, one who seems to flourish. The sufferer will be the larger community whose common life is endangered. Thus, for example, the commandment enjoining honor for one's father and mother has a promise attached: "that your days may be prolonged, and that it may go well with you, in the land which the LORD your God gives you." (Deut. 5:16). This does not mean that every disobedient son or disrespectful daughter must fail to flourish and will die at an early age. It means, rather, that no people can finally flourish if familial *pietas* is absent from their shared life.

This is in many ways an attractive theory — appealing in its simplicity and empirical grounding, and in the modesty with which it claims to do no more than establish minimal prescriptions for society. Appealing also in its recognition that we cannot always, by means of rational argument, persuade others to "see" what the natural law requires. The human will is disordered and, lacking certain virtues which only moral education can provide, we may not be in a position to see what the moral life requires. For that reason Aristotle said that ethics was a branch of politics and that only in a well-ordered society, in which virtue was inculcated, could one hope for the presence of proper moral vision.

We should, I think, be reluctant to adopt his view of government—a view that sees the task of government chiefly in educative terms, for those terms may miss the moral importance of freedom. But we cannot deny that a society must find ways, preferably through non-governmental structures and institutions, of shaping moral vision.

Granting that this theory of natural law is attractive, we must also admit, however, that it is minimal. It cannot by itself capture the fulness of "the good life," the richness and density that Christians have found in their way of life. This problem we might, of course, solve simply by addition—by enriching this minimal content with a more developed sense of the ways in which Christian faithfulness goes beyond natural law so understood. And, indeed, this is often precisely what we do. But the difficulties run still deeper, and they point us to an enduring tension for Christians between ethics (the good life in its rich density) and politics (where there may be much to be said for only minimal requirements). This type of natural law ethic may have considerable difficulty making place for self-sacrifice, for death in a good cause. For there may come a moment when what should be done if *I* want to survive is not what should be done if *we* want to survive. The courage society needs may be precisely the courage likely to get me killed. "Men need virtues as bees need stings. An individual bee may perish by stinging, all the same bees need stings; an individual man may perish by being brave or just, all the same men need courage and justice."[12] Hypothetical imperatives based on community survival may have a difficult time eliciting such a spirit of self-sacrifice and may, therefore, fall considerably short of forging a true communal bond. Behind the hypothetical imperative of "the political use of the law" always stands the implied threat: do this or else. And to make that threat effective we will need what government always needs: sanctions, the threat of force. Thus, however useful such a natural law ethic may be, it cannot capture successfully one of the great themes of the Christian life: self-giving and even self-sacrifice on behalf of the neighbor, done with a glad and willing heart.

II. A Fully Human Life

In seeking moral knowledge we might begin from a quite different sense of the natural: not what we regularly observe all around but the development appropriate to a particular kind of being. This is an evaluative rather than a descriptive category, and we will not gain this sort of knowledge simply by paying attention to regularities within the world. After all, more acorns lie on the ground and rot than grow into oak trees; yet, we still understand what it would mean to say that it is natural for the acorn to grow into an oak (or even, were we moved to put it this way, that the oak is the "flourishing" of the acorn). A society whose members courageously sacrifice themselves for each other may or may not survive for a long time, but in another sense it flourishes — as an image of what community at its best may be.

We can distinguish this version of natural law from the first by considering again the Decalog's requirement that children honor their parents. In terms of the first theory, this became in effect a hypothetical imperative: If a society wishes to perpetuate itself by asking the present generation to sacrifice itself for those who come after, it will need to inculcate in children a spirit of filial piety. Yet, important as such a claim is, it may seem to miss the sense in which a bond of parent and child is valued not simply as a means to communal survival but as the locus of cooperation and connection in which we first learn the meaning of love. This bond helps us to picture what human life at its best may be—to fall short of which is to risk not only our survival but the fulness of our humanity. From this perspective the requirements of the Decalog's second table are not simply minimal rules for community survival; they are an outline of faithfulness in a life that fully realizes its humanity.

Whatever problems may arise for this type of natural law ethic, it will at least have little difficulty justifying self-sacrifice. For on this view what matters is *how* we live, not *how long*. To realize our nature is not merely to survive, but to be a person of a certain sort. This approach may seem to capture the nobility of virtuous action better than the first, more modest and empirical, natural law theory. Perhaps for that very reason, however, it is far less likely to be a foundation for moral agreement. We may have great difficulty in specifying an ideal of human behavior and character that seems rationally demonstrable. How could we ever know what it means for human beings to flourish, to fully realize their nature? Nevertheless, Christians more than some others may be reluctant to give up on such a possibility; for the Christian understanding of our world as *creation* accounts for the difficulty of demonstrating such an ideal while, at the same time, giving us confidence that one may be found. In a passage of exquisite beauty and insight, Josef Pieper has made just this point.

> Because things come forth from the eye of God, they partake wholly of the nature of the Logos, that is, they are lucid and limpid to their very depths. It is their origin in the Logos which makes them knowable to men. But because of this very origin in the Logos, they mirror an *infinite* light and can therefore not be wholly comprehended. It is not darkness or chaos which makes them unfathomable. If a man, therefore, in his philosophical inquiry, gropes after the essence of things, he finds himself, by the very act of approaching his object, in an unfathomable abyss, but it is an abyss of *light*.[13]

What we learn is not best described as "partly true" (and, hence, "partly false"), but, at least sometimes, as "a part of the truth," which can remain true even as our understanding deepens and develops. As we come to know part of the truth about the meaning of faithfulness, we come upon not simply a work of our own making but the Creator's goal for the creation.

I do not wish to exaggerate the possibility of such rational discernment. The fact of human sinfulness must also affect our estimate of our own ability to know the full meaning of faithfulness. Since our loves are disordered, so may be our understanding. Unduly concerned with our own needs and interests, our vision of justice may be distorted. Too fearful to withstand the pressures of the workplace, we may fail to give our work the exacting attention it requires. Too eager to advance in that same work, we may fail to see obvious needs of our children. Lured by momentary pleasures or vanities, ruled by the desire to have our own way, we may ignore the needs of our spouse. It is hard to place much confidence in the judgments of people such as we know ourselves to be.

The deepest theological problem is not this, however; rather, it lies at the very heart of what Christians believe. How shall we articulate the meaning of a "flourishing" or "fully realized" human life apart from reference to Jesus? Christians have wanted to say that we become "mature" by growing "to the measure of the stature of the fulness of Christ."[14] But if the perfection of our humanity is revealed in Jesus, a Christian understanding of faithfulness within the spheres of worldly life may seem rather discontinuous with visions of human flourishing that come more naturally to us. This is, after all, a Jesus who must be in his Father's house even at some cost to the normal meaning of filial piety.[15] It is a Jesus whose notion of justice to those who labor may even seem unjust when measured by the light of our unaided reason.[16] And, more generally, Reinhold Niebuhr may have been right to characterize the love Jesus enacts as "a tangent toward 'eternity'" within time.[17] The perfection of human nature revealed in Jesus seems, at least sometimes, discontinuous with our natural understanding of human beings at their best.

Here is the theological issue to which either sort of natural law theory finally drives us: It is God who claims our faithfulness in the spheres of worldly life — his governance that we detect in the political use of the law, the goal of his creation that we discern at least in part when we learn a little about the meaning of faithfulness. That same God, however, in his redeeming action in Jesus, enacts a faithfulness that may seem different from what we think we have learned about the nature of virtue. If we affirm that it is the one God whose faithfulness is manifested both in his governance of creation and in the crucified Jesus, we must affirm both continuity and discontinuity in our understanding of the moral life. The worth and significance of faithfulness in the spheres of worldly life must be recognized; for there God sets before us the neighbors in need of our care. But the incompleteness of this life must also be seen and its ultimacy questioned; for in it God begins to school us for eternity, to shape our love into the form of his own faithfulness. The issue, finally, is Christological: The risen Christ *is* Jesus of Nazareth; yet the life to which he is raised is that of the new age. His resurrection *is* the vindication of the earthly life he lived among us; yet the life he now lives is not simply the natural completion or fulfillment of that life. From within that tension Christians reflect upon the meaning of faithfulness. It is the most fundamental limit to our search for understanding of the moral life.

III. Faith Seeking Understanding

In seeking moral understanding, therefore, Christians must begin from faith, though this starting point need not imply a wisdom available to them alone. Faith sees the governing hand of God at work in human communities when it discerns the minimal requirements for life together; faith discerns at least a part of God's own faithfulness when it gains insight into the meaning of morally mature human life. And we need not deny that what faith seeks it sometimes finds: understanding. Indeed, faith may broaden our vision and enable us to see what might otherwise have remained hidden to sight; it may enrich and enlarge our understanding of the moral life, and this enlarged understanding is, in principle at least, able to be shared with anyone and everyone. We have, for example, already seen the way in which faith's affirmation of the *person* of Christ was the motive force behind development of an enlarged understanding of human personhood. The search for such understanding is authorized by the Spirit of the risen Christ, whose resurrection vindicates and fulfills this life even while transcending it. Our natural reason is given a kind of modest affirmation, its vision is enlarged—but always within limits marked by discontinuity between this age and that to come.

Here we may add to the discussion of chapter one a different linguistic formula by which to characterize the problem of continuity and discontinuity between the moral life accessible to natural reason and the redeemed vision of one led by Christ's Spirit. That formula is the language of *ultimate* and *penultimate* by which Dietrich Bonhoeffer sought to affirm both the relative independence of natural reason and the ultimate grounding of all understanding in Christ, who is the wisdom of God.[18] This language provides a way to acknowledge the priority of God's redeeming work in Jesus, yet also affirm God's call to faithfulness within all the spheres of worldly life—and to affirm that call without absorbing it entirely within the life of faith. Bonhoeffer argues that we should begin from the end: with the ultimate. That last thing is God's compassion on sinners in Jesus. But within that particularity we find the world affirmed. Participation in Christ is ultimate because there is no more definitive word of God than that spoken in Jesus and no method for achieving what God gives freely in him. No amount of restructuring of this penultimate world can itself bring in the kingdom in which faithfulness is fully enacted. And yet, the significance of worldly life is not to be discounted. "A way must be traversed, even though, in fact, there is no way that leads to this goal. . . . The penultimate, therefore, remains even though the ultimate entirely annuls and invalidates it."[19]

Bonhoeffer is attempting both to affirm and negate our ordinary, garden-variety understandings of virtue in everyday life. These spheres must be distinguished from the kingdom of God, though not separated entirely from it. The penultimate—the flourishing of life within human history—is not the last thing, for it is *penul*timate. But for the sake of that last thing, human life must be preserved and nurtured, for it is pen*ultimate.* There is no way to advance from penultimate to ultimate—no way to move from the virtues we develop in worldly life to the faithful love that unites the body of Christ. Movement is in the other direction. "The penultimate shall be respected and validated for the sake of the approaching ultimate."[20] We can try to illustrate what Bonhoeffer has in mind by means of an illustration used by Helmut Thielicke. Since sickness and health— in their fullest senses—depend on whether we are at one with God, they are ultimately independent of the "psychophysical conditions with which medicine deals."[21] We might then wonder, however, what is the worth of the physician's calling and whether any real knowledge is available to physicians from the study of medicine alone. "It could be that someone whom I as a physician restore to health is thereby made more self-confident and goes to hell, whereas another whom I cannot help, who wastes away as I stand helplessly by,

takes his sickness as a visitation, the kind which brings
the prodigal home, and so wins through to eternity."[22]
What should we conclude? That medical knowledge is
of no worth or is no real knowledge at all? No. Only
that our understanding of its worth and working is
limited, that we cannot finally use it as a means toward
wholeness in the fullest sense, and that such final purposes always lie within the initiative of God alone.[23]
But even if there is no way from penultimate to ultimate, no way from medical healing to the wholeness
we truly need, such healing may still give us some
inkling or intimation of what we mean by wholeness
and what we hope for from God. The God who heals
our diseases is the God who forgives our iniquities and
crowns us with steadfast love and mercy.[24] The healing
he provides in the spheres of worldly life cannot be
entirely alien to his own ultimate purposes.

We can see, therefore. We can see and understand
a good bit about what is good and wise in this life, even
though we can never overcome or transcend the discontinuity that marks both the point of contact and the
point of rupture between God's creative and redeeming
action. In no sphere of life is this discontinuity more
evident than the political. There even more than elsewhere it may be difficult to discern even "intimations"
of continuity between the cities we struggle to preserve and the city God is building. Yet, if discontinuity
must be emphasized there, continuity (though perhaps
only visible to the eye of faith) must also not be denied.
An alluring example of this double movement is given
in Augustine's *City of God* by his use of the story of
the founding of Rome.

Romulus killed Remus, Augustine suggests, because
each "sought the glory of establishing the Roman
state," but this was a glory that could not be shared.[25]
Hence, conflict between them was inevitable, and we
should not suppose that such conflict can be eliminated
from human societies. Indeed, such conflicts only

demonstrate the extent to which our cities are per-
meated by *the* earthly city (the *civitas terrena*), since
it too was founded on a fratricide, when Cain killed
Abel. And conflict will continue to the end of history,
when the *civitas Dei* will be fully established.

But this is not Augustine's only use of the story of
Rome's founding. Much earlier in *City of God* Augustine
had also emphasized the discontinuity between earthly
politics and the *civitas Dei.* "As for this mortal life,
which ends after a few days' course, what does it matter
under whose rule a man lives, being so soon to die,
provided that the rulers do not force him to wicked and
impious acts?"[26] Christians should learn, Augustine
says, that if conquerors can endure many hardships for
the sake of earthly kingdoms, believers ought much
more be willing to endure hardship for the sake of a
heavenly one. Yet, in the midst of such an argument
designed to show the comparative unimportance of different political regimes, Augustine sounds a slightly
different note—appealing in a different way to the
story of Rome's founding. He suggests that "the re-
mission of sins . . . finds a kind of shadowy resemblance
in that refuge of Romulus, where the offer of impunity
for crimes of every kind collected a multitude which
was to result in the foundation of the city of Rome."[27]
Romulus is said to have founded Rome as a sanctuary
for criminals, and in that Augustine discerns a "shadowy resemblance," an imitation, of the peace offered
by the City of God. No path leads from intimation to
realization, but to have understood the meaning of
peace in the one is to have seen a shadowy resemblance
of the peace God finally gives.

7. Salvation and Politics, Church and Society

Our revels now are ended. These our actors,
As I foretold you, were all spirits and
Are melted into air, into thin air;
And, like the baseless fabric of this vision,
The cloud-capped towers, the gorgeous palaces,
The solemn temples, the great globe itself,
Yea, all which it inherit, shall dissolve,
And, like this insubstantial pageant faded,
Leave not a rack behind. We are such stuff
As dreams are made on, and our little life
Is rounded with a sleep.

Shakespeare, *The Tempest*

The work of God in history for our salvation, which begins with the call of Abraham, takes place within limits set in the primeval history of Genesis 1-11. The most fundamental of these limits is clear: No return to paradise is possible. Having fallen into the condition of sinfulness, human beings are no longer able to live in harmony with God or each other. A society governed solely by trust is not possible, and it is God's will that we should not attempt it. "He drove out the man; and at the east of the garden of Eden he placed the cherubim, and a flaming sword which turned every way, to guard the way to the tree of life" (Gen. 3:24). This does not mean that God withdraws his help and sustainingpower from humankind; indeed, when after their expulsion from the garden, Eve conceives a child by Adam, she says, "'I have gotten a man with the help of the LORD'" (Gen. 4:1). But God's help has in mind no return to the garden; it aims to preserve human life toward a saving work that will be fundamentally new and of which our own efforts can offer at best shadowy resemblances.

The limits of human life and the promise of God are reaffirmed in the story of the great flood. Because "every imagination of the thoughts of . . . [the human] heart was only evil continually . . . the LORD was sorry that he had made man on the earth . . . (Gen. 6:5-6). In the flood that is sent to blot out human wickedness from the earth, God spares Noah, who is said to have found favor in his eyes. It is clear, though, that in sparing Noah, God is, in fact, permitting the evil human heart to play out its history. For the covenant made with Noah after the waters have receded is one explicitly recognizing that human society cannot be based only on trust. And if the rainbow in the heavens is God's promise that he will no longer intervene so dramatically to remove evil from the earth, that promise can be made only because he has other plans for controlling wickedness. He will make positive use of the distrust that now affects human life, using force to control force. "Whoever sheds the blood of man, by man shall his blood be shed . . ." (Gen. 9:6).

That the limits of our possibilities must be taken seriously for as long as our history continues is made clear, finally, in the story of the Tower of Babel. In the land of Shinar were men of one language who thought they might fashion for themselves a united, consensual city. They proposed to build a tower with its top in the heavens—to make a name for themselves and to keep from being scattered and separated. When we consider the evil of the human heart, we know that such a plan could only have meant oppression for some and expanded power for others, not the construction of a har-

monious community. Their plan had to be stopped—
and God did so by confounding their languages and
scattering them over the face of the earth.

The limits therefore are clear: No return to paradise.
No human society free of distrust, free of the need for
force. No harmonious community achieved by free and
willing consent alone. Against the backdrop of these
truths political judgments must be made and human
societies ordered. This much we learn from a glance
backward in the story the Bible tells. Yet, that story
is oriented decisively toward the future God has promised, and we must look to that future if we wish to
understand fully the limits of politics.

I. Politics and Salvation

In looking to that future we should banish all forms—
revolutionary or evolutionary—of the old Christian
postmillenial dream of the kingdom on earth. The decisive *kairos* of God's kingdom is its presence in Jesus
of Nazareth, however scandalous such a claim may
seem.[1] There is no moving beyond that decisive moment, no greater gift that God will give than has been
given in Jesus the Christ, and the "now" that marks
the acceptable time and the day of salvation is every
"now" in which the word of Jesus is spoken.[2] Since no
more decisive moment is to be expected before the end
of our history, the Eternal confronts us in the word of
and about Jesus, and Augustine was correct to hold
that the millenial reign of the saints with Christ takes
place "from the first coming of Christ to the end of the
world."[3] From the time of Jesus of Nazareth to the end
of the age, human history is homogeneous. No decisively new turning point is to be expected.[4] Hence, we
must simply say with Augustine that in all our empirical communities both the *civitas Dei* and the *civitas
terrena* are "interwoven and mingled with one another."[5]

Just as Augustine was helped by this insight to draw back from his earlier Eusebian triumphalism — in which he had seen the extinction of paganism and the progress of Christian empire as the saving work of God — so we too should draw back from claiming decisive religious significance for any political achievement.[6] However deep our commitment to a particular people, however firm our belief that some ways of ordering a common life are better than others and more suited to offer at least a shadowy resemblance of what God has in store for the new creation, we should not say, as Cotton Mather did, that "New England has an Advocate in Heaven."[7] God has given his Christ, and nothing decisively new is to be anticipated within our history, which is, in Augustine's term, the *senectus mundi*, the senescence of our world.[8] All that remains is the manifestation — beyond history — of the kingdom that is Christ's, and for that day we cannot pave the way or discern the signs.[9] The recurring urge in Christian history to know those times and seasons, often expressed in terms of a third age of the spirit, has been rightly characterized by Eric Voegelin as one of "the first symptoms of the idea of a post-Christian era" — an attempt to go beyond the Christ God has given.[10]

Thus, the biblical story authorizes us to hope for the manifestation of Christ's rule that is the ultimate end toward which our penultimate history moves, but it authorizes only agnosticism about the course by which we move toward that end. Perhaps it is a measure of our own age's loss of faith that we tend to be agnostic or fearful about history's end while searching eagerly for signs that the kingdom can be built within our world. Paul Tillich, to whom we owe much of the contemporary interest in the concept of a political *kairos*, described it as "the moment in which the eternal breaks into the temporal, and the temporal is prepared to receive it."[11] Tillich held that the appearance of Jesus as the Christ was the one unique *kairos* of history but that "every turning-point in history in which the eternal judges and transforms the temporal" might also be called such a moment.[12] And perhaps so, if we were able to discern such moments as anything other than intimations or shadowy resemblances, as a way from penultimate to ultimate. But if we live within such limits, to attempt more is to "consecrate" a political cause or movement, to attach to it the name of Christ, and Tillich himself knew well the dangers that lay in wait. Writing in 1934 to Emanuel Hirsch, whose theological brilliance had been placed in service of the Nazi cause, Tillich asked whether Hirsch was not guilty of regarding current history as "a source of revelation alongside the biblical documents," and he wrote: "You have approximated the year 1933 so closely to the year 33, that it has gained for you the meaning of an event in the history of salvation."[13]

That is the key: When we recognize the limits of politics, we will not claim for political achievements — even ones as important as advancements of justice or freedom — the status of events in the history of salvation. Hence, however wide the gap between the justice of their respective causes, we should not fail to see the connection between Hirsch's claims and Gustavo Gutierrez's contention that the present moment in Latin America is a *kairos*, "a moment of heightened revelation both of God and of new paths on the journey of fidelity to the word of God."[14] Theological danger is near at hand when one writes, as Gutierrez does: "Of this situation we may say with Paul: 'Now is the favorable time; this is the day of salvation. . . .'"[15]

It is possible, however, to connect closely political liberation and the biblical story without attempting to make political goals constitutive of salvation. In a richly rewarding interpretation, Michael Walzer has read the Exodus story as "a paradigm of revolutionary politics."[16] He argues that the story "is plausibly understood in political terms, as a liberation and a revolu-

tion."[17] Central to the story's development is what
happens to the people as they march to the promised
land. It is important for Walzer that the march be
understood properly—to the promised land, but neither back to paradise nor forward to a messianic kingdom. He distinguishes an Exodus politics, which seeks
neither to force the coming of the last days nor return
to the lost garden, from political messianism, which
hopes for an end to history as we know it. The radical
politics for which the Exodus story is paradigmatic is,
therefore, a gradualist one, and its worth for Walzer
lies chiefly in the moral transformation that takes place
along the way through the wilderness. To read the story
rightly is to reject the hope for a return to paradise
and to realize that even the promised land (which will
still resemble Egypt in many ways) is not as important
as the sense we develop of ourselves as a people, and
the moral transformation that disciplined devotion to
the cause makes possible. The ideal is not primarily
milk and honey in the promised land, but the holiness
and virtue of a transformed people—in the biblical language, "a kingdom of priests."[18]

Thus Walzer takes account in some ways of the limits
of politics while still reading the Exodus—so central
in the story of salvation—as essentially an act of political liberation. But he avoids utopianism—or, in the
language of religion, avoids the "consecration" of any
political cause—chiefly by reading the story as a human
undertaking, a political deliverance from which the
hand of God is largely absent. Christian political
thought cannot, however, bracket God; it must, by contrast, take the Exodus story up into a larger context
in which the story of Jesus is central. Michael Goldberg,
without bracketing God in the way Walzer's reading
does, has still insightfully distinguished the Jewish
master story (of the Exodus) from the Christian master
story (of Jesus' passion-resurrection).[19] Throughout the
Jewish master story the chief demand is Moses' reit-

erated word to Pharaoh: "Let my people go!" Political
liberation for his people is the aim even of God's action.
In the Christian master story, however, repentance becomes the chief goal. The enemy is no longer any political Pharaoh. The enemy is nearer at hand: the sinful
people themselves.[20] Because Jesus' cross and resurrection is the act by which God creates sinful humankind anew, it is also the death of human striving to
achieve the saving purposes of God within history.

Walzer himself notes that Christian revolutionaries
who have read the Exodus story as he does—chiefly
English Puritans and some contemporary liberation
theologians—"are plausibly called judaizers: they defend the 'carnality' of the promise; they seek a worldly
kingdom."[21] By contrast, we should not shrink from
asserting that a proper *Christian* reading will "spiri-
tualize" the promise. The deliverance God has in mind
for his creation goes beyond anything we should expect
in our history and is achieved not by political power
but by the powerlessness of the cross. Such a view can
be charged with creating Christians who are passive,
acquiescent citizens, and perhaps this may sometimes
be its psychological effect. Reinhold Niebuhr was probably correct to note that when we heighten the religious
tension in this way—by refusing to view any political
achievement as a means to advance the coming of the
kingdom—we make it psychologically difficult to sustain the moral tension from which decent action flows.[22]
But such passivity need not result. That the City God
is building will not be achieved within human history
or produced by political progress does not mean that
every small achievement along the way is of no consequence—even to God. Such steps are, after all, pen-
ultimate, and whatever serves human need rightly
claims our attention and care. If a "spiritualized" understanding of the kingdom has sometimes produced
acquiescent citizens, the opposite may as easily result.
Those who are never fully at home in any historical

community may settle down passively, content to wait for the deliverance God will work beyond history, but the hope they place in God will also sustain many penultimate, political commitments. They cannot be trusted to be docile citizens, for theirs is a divided loyalty.

This means that the roots of our modern liberal society must be traced not only to the masterless men of whom Hobbes wrote or the commercial men whom Tocqueville analyzed but also to Christian belief. The theological premises are evident in Augustine's *City of God*. Rejecting Cicero's understanding of a commonwealth as a people "united in association by a common sense of right and a community of interest," Augustine proposes to demythologize the sphere of political history (even as nature had been desacralized in Hebrew and Christian thought). He suggests that a people is simply "the association of a multitude of rational beings united by a common agreement on the objects of their love."[23] Such a definition permits us to recognize common interests, to distinguish better and worse peoples according to the nature of their shared interests, and even to see in some shared interests what may be an intimation of the City of God. But at the same time it diminishes our expectations and lowers the stakes in the game of politics. We might translate Augustine's intent in this way: From a sphere that exists only by making positive use of distrust and force, we should not seek the depth of common purpose or the sense of intimacy and belonging necessary to secure our identity at its deepest level.

II. Religion and Public Life

A politics of limited expectations means, then, a politics that is not a vehicle for our religious aspirations. It means a church which does not think itself responsible for sustaining the political community. But it need not mean a public life in which religion plays no part. Indeed, from two quite different perspectives one might claim that religion cannot be excluded from the public sphere.

We might suggest, first, that it will be very difficult to describe any societally shared morality—any code of civic righteousness—that can be sealed off from religion. Moral agreement that penetrates no further than the rules of the game, rules which govern how individuals may pursue their private interests in public, is not objectionable, but it is probably impossible to attain in undiluted form. The story of many Western societies during the modern era is one of continuing attempts to fashion such agreement—attempts motivated in large measure by a desire to escape the destructive consequences of a life in which minimal civility was deemed insufficient. The intangible goods of the older orders were not without their allure—the glory of the king and honor of the nobles, the public good which citizens of antiquity vied with each other to serve, the salvation to which Christians gave complete devotion.[24] But these religious and quasi-religious visions of perfection—beyond the reach of many and often the focus of intense disagreement—were costly. The attempt to reach a shared vision of *the* good life did not always seem to serve immediate human needs, and many people gladly turned to commercial republics which settled for agreement on the rules of the game and banished visions of the good life to more private spheres.[25]

That move is understandable. To it we owe much that is attractive in our way of life. But the division between public morality and private religious belief, which this move seeks to entrench, can never be definitively established or secured. Public life is a conversation in which the line is drawn and redrawn, but never firmly fixed. A nice illustration of this is available in a letter written by Baptist theologian Roger

Williams to the town of Providence in January 1655. Williams was a great defender of liberty of conscience, but he writes here to defend himself against the suggestion that the liberty for which he had argued was detrimental to public life. He offers an illustration.

> I shall at present propose only this case: There goes many a ship to sea, with many hundred souls in one ship, whose weal and woe is common, and is a true picture of a commonwealth, or a human combination or society. It hath fallen out sometimes, that both papists and protestants, Jews and Turks, may be embarked in one ship; upon which supposal I affirm, that all the liberty of conscience that ever I pleaded for, turns upon these two hinges — that none of the papists, protestants, Jews, or Turks, be forced to come to the ship's prayers or worship, nor compelled from their own particular prayers or worship, if they practice any.[26]

This much, he held, the common life should neither exact nor control. But it is striking to note what Williams goes on to permit. The commander of the ship, who is responsible for governing the ship's course, must require "justice, peace and sobriety" of all. Any who "refuse to help, in person or purse, toward the common charges or defence" may be compelled and punished. It would also be proper to punish and resist any who "preach or write that there ought to be no commanders or officers, because all are equal in Christ." One begins to wonder whether Williams's distinction between public and private can work. Religious beliefs may influence our vision of justice, our convictions about the appropriateness of common defense, our commitment to various understandings of human equality. If certain dogmas or rituals can perhaps be confined to the private realm, the life to which they give rise, together with the virtues it commends and the vices it condemns, cannot be so confined. In short, religious belief will impinge on public life in countless ways. It can be banished from the public realm only by those unwilling to continue the conversation in which the line between public and private is constantly drawn and redrawn.

But a willingness to continue that conversation indefinitely is precisely what a minimal understanding of public morality requires! It is the mark of a liberal polity. Hence, it is a mistake, though a historically understandable one, to think that Western liberal societies must be characterized by a commitment to banish from public life all religious visions of the good life. Their commitment, rather, is to continuing conversation about what should be private and what is legitimately public. Sustaining that conversation is a fragile and precarious undertaking. There may even be moments when it cannot and should not be sustained, when the claims of moral vision outweigh those of political prudence. But the costs of such social breakdown, even if necessary and right, are likely to be great; the vision of Lincoln did not triumph apart from the generalship of Grant.

There is also a second, quite different, perspective from which one might try to make place for religion within the public sphere. We could make room not for particular convictions of particular communities of believers but for a shared civil religion: a religion as minimal as the public morality it is meant to undergird. Rousseau, who was perhaps the most influential and penetrating theorist of civil religion, believed that no community could survive without some shared religious underpinnings; yet he also argued that *Christian* belief could not provide the needed support. Its vision of the good life cannot be domesticated within the public sphere. It is, he wrote, a religion "which gives men two legislative orders, two rulers, two homelands, puts them under two contradictory obligations, and prevents their being at the same time both churchmen and citizens." [27] If we think Rousseau's claims too absolute, we need only say that Christianity makes such divided loyalty an ever-present possibility — hence, on Rousseau's terms, constitutes a danger to the body politic. "Everything that destroys social unity is worthless, and all institutions that set man at odds with himself are worthless."[28] Of course, Christians themselves recognize the tension to which Rousseau points, but they hold that it must be suffered within human history, that we must learn to live politically with divided loyalties. Rousseau, however, hoped for a greater deliverance than that; his was not a politics of limited expectations. "Whoever ventures on the enterprise of setting up a people must be ready, shall we say, to change human nature, to transform each individual, who by himself is entirely complete and solitary, into a part of a much greater whole, from which that same individual will then receive, in a sense, his life and his being."[29]

Because that was his concept of the political task, Rousseau did not give up hope for a civil religion that might function better than Christianity. Indeed, precisely because politics was a sphere in which the transformation of human nature was to be attempted, it could not get along without the help of religion. Only shared religious beliefs and public rituals could provide the bonds necessary to hold a society together. Religious dogmas are not necessary, but the sentiments of sociability associated with them are. The teachings of the domesticated civil religion could, therefore, be

> simple and few in number, expressed precisely and without explanations or commentaries. The existence of an omnipotent, intelligent, benevolent divinity that foresees and provides; the life to come; the happiness of the just; the punishment of sinners; the sanctity of the social contract and the law — these are the positive dogmas. As for the negative dogmas, I would limit them to a single one: no intolerance.[30]

This is a civil religion minimal enough to cause no disturbance, one that does not champion any potentially divisive vision of the good life. But, still, a religion that might help a civilization to endure.

Whatever the extravagances of his theorizing, Rousseau sees clearly why those concerned for the health of public communities are often drawn to speak of the need for something like a civil religion. They seek common purposes and common causes in which people may lose and then find themselves — and in that way experience the transformation of self that Rousseau describes, a conversion from the isolation of individual pursuits to a sense of oneness and belonging. They seek to transcend the confusion and pluralism of our moral languages and make incarnate in our public life some shared vision. But for Christian thought the purpose of public life should be neither the transformation of human nature nor the overcoming of our divided loyalties. The public sphere is not to claim the whole of our being. Its purpose is to make possible a continuing conversation — a time in which, first of all, the word of God's mercy may be spoken; a time also in which we may explore and seek to expand the interests we hold in common. And as long as that conversation continues, we can be confident that — whatever the vices of our liberal, individualistic, commercial society — some shared moral vision continues to exist among us. Even within a band of robbers, Augustine noted, there must be some justice, however rough, if they are to remain a band.[31] Small comfort, perhaps, if our dreams are anything like Rousseau's, but considerable solace if we long for that City whose builder and maker is God. It is better, therefore, to set aside the dream of civil religion and affirm instead the rightful participation of particular communities of belief in the continuing conversation through which we specify the meaning of civic righteousness in our community.

III. Church and Society

The church is constituted and continually reconstituted only by the gospel: the word that in Jesus of

Nazareth God has made peace with us. To speak that word, to proclaim the gospel, is therefore always the essential task of the church. That proclamation continually renews and extends the church. Where that word is spoken the church is present.

In our own time this way of characterizing the nature and mission of the church has seemed inadequate to some, who find in it too little emphasis on a social or political mission of the church. In a sentence that has given rise to much debate, the Second General Assembly of the Synod of Bishops of the Roman Catholic Church seemed to make a political mission constitutive of the church's identity. In "Justice in the World," a document issued in 1971, the bishops stated: "Action on behalf of justice and participation in the transformation of the world fully appear to us as a constitutive dimension of the preaching of the Gospel, or, in other words, of the Church's mission for the redemption of the human race and its liberation from every oppressive situation."[32] The apostolic exhortation *Evangelii Nuntiandi*, issued by Pope Paul VI after the next general assembly of the Synod of Bishops in 1974, appeared more cautious, warning frequently against the temptation to "reduce" the church's mission "to the dimensions of a simply temporal project."[33] The exhortation does say that the church "has the duty to proclaim the liberation of millions of human beings," and that such work "is not foreign to evangelization."[34] But many activities that are not constitutive of the church's identity may also not be foreign to its mission. What constitutes the church is now described in a passage like the following:

> For the Church, evangelizing means bringing the good news into all the strata of humanity, and through its influence transforming humanity from within and making it new.... But there is no new humanity if there are not first of all new persons renewed by baptism and by lives lived according to the gospel. The purpose of evangeli-

zation is therefore precisely this interior change, and if it has to be expressed in one sentence the best way of stating it would be to say that the Church evangelizes when she seeks to convert, solely through the divine power of the message she proclaims, both the personal and collective consciences of people, the activities in which they engage, and the lives and concrete milieux which are theirs.[35]

This is what the exhortation calls "the grace and vocation proper to the Church, her deepest identity."[36]

For my purposes, of course, the fundamental issue is not the proper exegesis of these documents but the question they take up: What constitutes the church, its identity and mission? Francis Schüssler Fiorenza has argued that a social and political mission is as intrinsic to the church's identity as its efforts in education and health care, and, of course, the church has very actively formed its own education and healing institutions. One might reply that the church has done this because the larger society failed to meet such needs, but Fiorenza does not think this captures fully the reasons for the church's involvement in this work.

> Catholics did not establish universities and schools only as substitutive institutions until the state could take them over. They never doubted that schools and hospitals were integral to the Church's mission. Moreover, if taken to its ultimate consequences, a substitutional theory would result in the Church's removal from welfare activities, hospitals, hospices, and educational institutions, would limit it to liturgical celebration, proclamation, catechesis.[37]

I confess my inability to find such an upshot disturbing, though, of course, I do think it very unlikely. But if, in fact, a society were so ordered that its educational and healing institutions took serious account of our relation to God, if its poor and needy were met with concern and care — if, that is, we lived in something that might warrant the name Christendom! — then a church that devoted itself to "liturgical celebration, proclamation,

[and] catechesis" would be no cause for worry. Such a church would be free in ways it seldom is today to live by and from the word. It could devote itself to "the equipment of the saints" for their countless vocations,[38] and it would be free of the unseemly clericalism that has so often marred its history.

Such a day will never come in human history, of course, and the church's mission to society should not be defined as if it might. In our world much that passes for education will ignore the true Light that enlightens our intellects; much that is considered healing will not include the relation with God which alone can make us whole. Hence, it is no surprise that at many different times and places the church should have seen these functions as important for its mission in the world— though we should note that it does so not by taking over "secular" educational or healing institutions but by seeking its own place within them and, at the same time, establishing its own institutions devoted to learning and health. The analogy suggests that the church best carries out a social mission by seeking ways to contribute to society's efforts to care for the needy and by itself living as a standing alternative to the ways in which our communities are ordered and governed— but not by supposing that it has a word by which this world should be governed.

Hence, the church is constituted only by the word of the gospel, and to speak that word is its essential task. What is essential need not be exhaustive, however, and the church also quite properly understands itself as having a social mission. If the contours of Christian life are those sketched in chapter one, this mission will be carried out in the face of twin temptations: to attempt a Christian restructuring of society (the Eusebian temptation, leading inevitably to a cultural Christianity), or to deny that any common ground can be found in the political sphere (the sectarian temptation). Each of these in different ways would divide the body of Christ, consume the bulk of the church's resources in the task of structuring (either political or churchly) community, and turn Jesus into a new lawgiver. And if the moral theory outlined earlier is sound, such a mission must focus more on the *right* than the *good* — on specific needs and injustices, rather than large-scale plans for social transformation. But, fundamentally, faith must be active in love, and love, in turn, must seek justice for the neighbor. Hence, in its social mission the church engages in works of mercy that serve human need and works of witness that condemn injustice.

Flowing from faith created by the gospel, the corporal works of mercy — feeding the hungry, giving drink to the thirsty, visiting the sick, burying the dead, clothing the naked, welcoming the stranger, and visiting the imprisoned — have been central in the church's life.[39] The fourth-century Roman Emperor Julian — whom Christians termed "apostate" for his attempts to revive paganism — ordered his imperial clergy to imitate Christians by providing charitable relief for the poor, noting that "the impious Galileans support not only their own poor, but ours as well."[40] And the historian Paul Johnson has written that in the first centuries of its existence the church "ran a miniature welfare state in an empire which for the most part lacked social services."[41]

Such giving and receiving is grounded in the most basic affirmations of Christian faith. The being of the Triune God is from eternity one in which the Father gives life to the Son, who, receiving that life, offers it back to the Father through the Spirit. And the same principle of exchange marks God's external work — the exchange between Christ and sinners, in which he bears the guilt and endures the cross, and they receive freedom and life. This is what God is like — and into that divine life Christians are drawn when they become members of Christ's body. Hence, when St. Paul wanted to encourage the Corinthians to contribute to the offering he was gathering for relief of the poor in Jerusalem, he appealed precisely to this theological ground: "You know the grace of our Lord Jesus Christ, that though he was rich, yet for your sake he became poor, so that by his poverty you might become rich" (2 Cor. 8:9). The goal is not sharing, but giving and receiving. "I do not mean that others should be eased and you burdened, but that as a matter of equality your abundance at the present time should supply their want, so that their abundance may supply your want, that there may be equality" (2 Cor. 8:13-14). The specific tasks included in the church's works of mercy may vary from place to place. Where others—for example, government—provide service, the church may preserve its resources. Nor need such work be done in any particular way. However it is done, through whatever institutional channels the church carries out this mission, works of mercy will remain essential in the common life of the church. Such service begins first within the body of Christ, but it extends to all in need of care.[42]

There is always a certain danger in placing strong emphasis upon the church's works of mercy, especially given the enormous scope of human need in our world. The danger is that the church's life will be overwhelmed by its efforts to organize and offer care, and then the proclamation of the gospel, by which the church lives and is nourished, may lose its centrality. Against such danger there is no protection other than self-conscious attention to that word which constitutes the church. The possibility of abuse must not, however, lead us to deny the essential nature of the church's works of mercy. Faith must be active in love.

Love, in turn, must seek justice, and in addition to its works of mercy the church is also called to bear witness against injustice. As care for those in need flows out of the church's central task of proclamation (since the faith created by the gospel is active in love), so also the work of witness is connected — though less directly — to the gospel. When in human societies God provides liberty, justice, and peace, he does what is *pen*ultimate and does not thereby create the kingdom of Christ. But in thus preserving human life toward the day when his kingdom will be manifested beyond our history, he does what is pen*ultimate* — and what cannot, therefore, be unrelated to the gospel. It is the one loving God who carries on constant struggle against Satan both in the church's preaching of the gospel and in the church's witness against injustice — one struggle, against a single opponent, waged by the God who in all that he does is love, waged in two different but related ways.

Gustaf Aulen has nicely summarized the responsibility of the church to bear such political witness. Although the state is "the bearer of God's law as the preserver of an order of justice," government may fail in this task. "Power may become the master of justice instead of its servant," and then the church must speak. "Under such circumstances the church must function as the conscience of the state. It cannot avoid this obligation, because it is its duty to watch over the sanctity of God's law."[43] But the church bears its witness through the only power entrusted to it — the power to speak God's word. "The role which the church maintains in this kind of conflict must be characterized by its own function. The struggle must be carried on entirely with the church's own spiritual weapons."[44]

Just as there are dangers in the church's commitment to works of mercy, so too there are dangers in its commitment to a mission of witness. In part the danger is the same: The energy and resources of the church can be consumed in political witness, the gospel lose its centrality, and the church fail to be renewed by the word which ever constitutes it anew. In addition, however, the church's work of witness may involve a peculiar temptation — the tempation to say more than the church is authorized to do. Max Stackhouse has noted that, although the Christian faith clearly demands *praxis*, "it cannot easily be said to involve any specific orthopraxy at all."[45] To be sure, certain actions have been understood as clear violations of the faith, and Stackhouse offers examples: burning incense to Caesar, deceitfully using the church's resources for one's personal benefit, selling indulgences, slaughtering Jews in the name of Christ, burning witches and engaging in bloody crusades, establishing racial segregation on purportedly Christian grounds, relegating women to second-class status. But these are negative examples — cases of *in*justice. By contrast, "[i]t cannot be said that there is one and only one orthopraxy with regard to handling financial matters, giving to Caesar what is properly Caesar's, dealing with forgiveness, or structuring social-political life to include pluralistic groups."[46] Any program of distributive justice within a society must involve the balancing of many competing goods and goals within that common life, and there may be many different — and acceptable — ways of achieving such balance. No one of them can be characterized as the Christian vision for society. For this reason Helmut Thielicke has characterized the church's work of witness as the office of a watchman — not provider of a plan for social reconstruction, but a witness against injustice.[47] The temptation to say more is very probably the temptation to exercise political rule.

Even if the church's work of witness has no single vision to set forth for society, even if its witness is chiefly negative in character, we should not doubt that where its works of mercy and witness are faithfully carried out a community characterized by giving and receiving — an intimation of the city of promise — will be more closely approximated. If that is not always evident to sight, faith can affirm it even while struggling to remain faithful in the church's mission to society.

8. Mortality:
The Measure of Our Days

Men must endure
Their going hence, even as their coming hither;
Ripeness is all.

Shakespeare, *King Lear*

For much of human history death was associated at least as much with infancy and youth as with old age. To live to be old was an achievement — a modest victory over death, and one often thought of in religious terms as a blessing.[1] In our time, however, when death and old age so often go hand in hand, to grow old becomes cause for fear and worry, not for rejoicing. But this suggests that our deepest problem is not that we grow old. It is, rather, that we die. In some ways we might even say that the preoccupation of our culture with the different stages of life and with growing old is simply one more mechanism for "the denial of death."[2] Harold Moody has written that the idea of life-span development, given us by psychology, is "the great and indispensable myth of our time."[3] Indispensable — because it gives us a way of trying to see our life whole and entire, as significant and meaningful. But it is also a great myth — needed to help us build a dike that holds back recognition of our mortality. It is not easy to say with the psalmist:

151

> Lord, let me know my end,
>   and what is the measure of my days;
>   let me know how fleeting my life is!
>   (Psalm 34:4)

Yet, acquiring such knowledge is the fundamental task of each of us.

To think about our death means also, of course, to think about our life—what it means to be a human being, what sort of nature and life we share. To be sure, these are large themes, and they have been treated by many authors in many books. By considering just three of the most profound of these books, we can begin to see the range of possible attitudes toward death.

I. Stories of Death

In *Charlotte's Web*, by E. B. White, we read of one who dies alone, but who also lives on in her offspring.[4] Charlotte is an exceptional spider whose affection as a friend and talent as a writer have saved the pig Wilbur from becoming ham and pork chops. Wilbur has even been judged a prize pig at the fair. But when the fair is over and preparations are being made to return Wilbur to the Zuckerman's farm, Charlotte tells him that she will not be returning with him. Having created her masterpiece, her egg sac with 514 eggs, she knows that her strength is spent and that she will soon die. Panic-stricken at the news, Wilbur manages at least to take the egg sac back with him, carrying it in his mouth on the journey home.

As Wilbur is loaded for the return trip, Charlotte whispers good-bye, content in the knowledge that her children are safe.

> She never moved again. Next day, as the Ferris wheel was being taken apart and the race horses were being loaded into vans and the entertainers were packing up

their belongings and driving away in their trailers, Charlotte died. The Fair Grounds were soon deserted. The sheds and buildings were empty and forlorn. . . . No one was with her when she died. (p. 171)

In this description of Charlotte's death we do not fail to hear the loneliness, the sadness, and the drabness of death. What is there in the story for us to set against these terrors? Two things chiefly. First, there is friendship. When Wilbur wonders why Charlotte has done so much for him, spinning the webs whose messages garnered for him the reputation as a prize pig, Charlotte responds by pointing to the reciprocal benefits of their friendship.

"You have been my friend," replied Charlotte. "That in itself is a tremendous thing. I wove my webs for you because I liked you. After all, what's a life anyway? We're born, we live a little while, we die. A spider's life can't help being something of a mess, with all this trapping and eating flies. By helping you, perhaps I was trying to lift up my life a trifle." (p. 164)

If we read this as more than a book about spiders and pigs, we can detect here a vision that might be called Aristotelian. Caught up in the messiness of life, in search of a brief flourishing before we are replaced by others essentially like us, we are most ourselves when united in a bond of friendship. Together we take the measure of our days, and in so doing we achieve a certain nobility.

More than that should not be asked, since the cycle of nature is greater than we are, and in its own way it offers us a chance of victory over mortality. Charlotte tells Wilbur:

"These autumn days will shorten and grow cold. The leaves will shake loose from the trees and fall. Christmas will come, then the snows of winter. You will live to enjoy the beauty of the frozen world. . . . Winter will pass, the days will lengthen, the ice will melt in the pasture pond.

The song sparrow will return and sing, the frogs will awake, the warm wind will blow again. All these sights and sounds and smells will be yours to enjoy, Wilbur — this lovely world, these precious days...." (pp. 163f.)

Wilbur has been saved from a premature death at the butcher's hands — not that he may never die, but that he may live out his life in full as Charlotte has. And Charlotte, in turn, lives on in her children. Wilbur has taken the egg sac back with him, and one fine spring morning the little spiders begin to crawl out. In a few days there comes a "warm draft of rising air" that carries off one after another of the young spiders. In despair at losing Charlotte's children, Wilbur cries himself to sleep. But when he wakes, he discovers that three of Charlotte's daughters have stayed behind to live in the barn and be his friends. Although Wilbur always remembers Charlotte with special love, he is greatly pleased with his new companions. Charlotte has not herself survived, but her life has pointed beyond itself through the continuation of the species. Her willingness to wither and die has given rise to the next generation.

There are, however, other ways to face death, and *Charlotte's Web* is not the only child's book that will bear many readings. Another is Felix Salten's *Bambi* — translated into English by Whittaker Chambers and described in John Galsworthy's Foreword as "a little masterpiece."[5] If E. B. White was our Aristotle, it would not be far from the mark to think of Salten as our Seneca or Marcus Aurelius.

The story of Bambi is really about one thing: The young deer Bambi is gradually taught by the old stag how to live wisely, and much of what he learns has to do with death. Bambi and his mother take a walk, he sees the ferret kill a mouse, and his mother has no answer when he asks, "Why?" He learns that they can play in the meadow safely only after dark. And he learns from inanimate nature as the leaves begin slowly to fall from the trees.

Gradually Bambi's mother leaves him alone more and more. Missing her, he wanders through the forest, calling her name. On one such occasion he encounters the old stag for the first time. "What are you crying about?" asks the old stag. "Can't you stay by yourself?" (p. 81). And, indeed, this is the essence of the wisdom passed on to Bambi by the old stag: that he must "act bravely" and, still more, that he must live alone.

> When he was still a child the old stag had taught him that you must live alone. Then and afterwards the old stag had revealed much wisdom and many secrets to him. But of all his teachings this had been the most important; you must live alone, if you wanted to preserve yourself, if you understood existence, if you wanted to attain wisdom, you had to live alone. (p. 268)

The ordinary emotional ties that bind one to another, however sweetly they may draw us, are dangerous. Drawn by them we cease to live within ourselves and become vulnerable. One day Bambi thinks he hears Faline calling him, and, overcome with desire to be near her, he begins running toward the voice. Suddenly the old stag is there, barring his way. Frantic to see Faline, Bambi tries to persuade the old stag to let him go to her, but the old stag insists that "she isn't calling" and "it isn't she" (p. 185). But Bambi must go, and so the old stag leads him cautiously by a roundabout way until, from the safety of cover, Bambi sees a hunter imitating Faline's call. The lesson is a clear one, even if painful to learn: Bambi is most vulnerable when he does not live within himself.

The dangers and hardships of life become occasions for learning how to live. And only those who learn can flourish. When Gobo thinks of winter and the difficulty of finding food, he says: "It must be dreadful." To which Bambi responds: "It isn't dreadful. It's only hard"

(p. 227). But Gobo had for a time been cared for by a hunter—pampered like a domestic animal, fed, but made to wear a halter. After Gobo had returned to the forest animals, congratulating himself on his friendship with humans, it had been the old stag who noticed the halter still around his neck and said: "You poor thing" (p. 210). Gobo had not learned to live within himself, to use the hardships of life and the death to which it leads as training in virtue. Lacking such wisdom he could not possess the inner freedom which can face with tranquillity external hardship and even death. This is the wisdom of the old stag: that we must learn to live alone and that in death "we are all alone" (p. 287).

To live well one must know how to die well. The old stag is like Seneca's sage: he has such "confidence in himself" (*fiducia sui!*) that he does not retreat from whatever fortune may bring.

> Nor has he any reason to fear her, for he counts not merely his chattels and his possessions and his position, but even his body and his eyes and his hand and all else that makes life very dear to a man, nay, even himself, among the things that are given on sufferance, and he lives as one who has been lent to himself and will return everything without sorrow when it is reclaimed.[6]

The good man cannot be harmed by ill fortune, not even by death, for he has learned to live within himself and to think nothing good except virtue itself. Even death, finally, cannot touch him.

I do not know for certain how we weigh these matters or make these judgments, but, speaking only for myself, I must say that *Bambi* is a more profound book than *Charlotte's Web*, probing more deeply the mystery of mortality. But still better is the third story I take up here: *The Last Battle*, by C. S. Lewis.[7] Last of the seven Chronicles of Narnia, it recounts the end of Narnia and the entry into "Aslan's country" of all loyal Narnians.

From the very outset of the story, readers know what is inevitably to come. Chapter 1 begins: "In the last days of Narnia . . ." The first sentence of chapter 2 introduces Tirian, "last of the Kings of Narnia." And the central characters know what Jewel the Unicorn puts succinctly: "all worlds draw to an end; except Aslan's own country" (p. 84). Hence, there is plenty of room in Narnia for a nobility which the old stag would understand well. When Calormene soldiers infiltrate the land through treachery, Tirian sends Roonwit the Centaur in search of help and reinforcements. But Roonwit finds the other Narnians already killed or captured and himself takes a fatal arrow in the side. Farsight the Eagle brings to Tirian Roonwit's last message: "I was with him in the last hour and he gave me this message to your Majesty: to remember that all worlds draw to an end and that noble death is a treasure which no one is too poor to buy" (p. 86).

That all worlds end is not simply the result of a natural process. It is ultimately the will and work of Aslan. And, more particularly, when "night falls on Narnia," it is because Aslan says: "Now make an end" (p. 149). And against such an ending we are not to protect ourselves. The pain that emotional attachment brings must be risked out of love for the goodness of Narnia. When Narnia is no more, the children who had been sent to help faithful Narnians are called "further in and further up" into Aslan's country.

> "So," said Peter. "Night falls on Narnia. What, Lucy! You're not *crying*? With Aslan ahead, and all of us here?"
>
> "Don't try to stop me, Peter," said Lucy. "I am sure Aslan would not. I am sure it is not wrong to mourn for Narnia. Think of all that lies dead and frozen behind that door." . . .
>
> "Sirs," said Tirian, "The ladies do well to weep. See I do so myself. I have seen my mother's death. What world but Narnia have I ever known? It were no virtue, but great discourtesy if we did not mourn." (pp. 149f.)

Like Charlotte and Wilbur, Narnians have found much to delight in and much to cherish in their world. But knowing that all worlds except Aslan's country come to an end, they cannot find sufficient meaning and purpose simply in the succession of Narnian generations — all of which, after all, lead toward a *finis*.[8] Succession of time and generations, however long extended, does not itself offer a certain kind of present significance.[9] It offers quantity and continuance — more of the same — when what we desire is something qualitatively different. Hence, even if we overcame aging and death we would not have achieved the heart's desire; for the desire for God is not a longing for more of this life. The old stag, of course, had seen this but was driven to conclude that we dare not therefore attach ourselves to the beauty of this world and the delights of companionship.

What *The Last Battle* offers is a story that legitimizes and invites our attachment to this world, accepts even the pain such attachment may bring, and does not pretend that the death which ends all such attachment is not dreadful. It pictures for us creatures whose hearts are quite rightly tied to particular places and persons, who are finite and who must reckon with the passing of time, but creatures who also are made to desire something more. Not just more of the same, but the qualitatively different country of Aslan. Such creatures — who belong *both* in Narnia *and* Aslan's country, and who must simply learn to live with such dual membership — are the object of Christian vision. They are dust of the ground and truly belong to this finite world. They are free spirits, made for God and transcending the finite realm. For them death itself must be ambivalent, as ambivalent as the stable door through which the last Narnians are driven by the Calormenes.

"I feel in my bones," said Poggin, "that we shall all, one by one, pass through that dark door before morning. I can think of a hundred deaths I would rather have died."

"It is indeed a grim door," said Tirian. "It is more like a mouth."

"Oh, can't we do *anything* to stop it?" said Jill in a shaken voice.

"Nay, fair friend," said Jewel, nosing her gently. "It may be for us the door to Aslan's country and we shall sup at his table tonight." (p. 120)

As the natural end of temporal existence in Narnia, death was always to be anticipated and accepted with as much nobility as one could muster. Like Jewel, Narnians can hope in Aslan, but such hope is not sight, and it would be presumptuous to think of the object of hope as if it were one's present possession. Hence, death remains fearful. And for those who carry dual membership, it becomes doubly dreadful. It threatens the loss of Narnia. And it seems, at least, to bring to an end the quest for Aslan's country, the deepest longing of the heart.

II. Christian Vision and the Ambivalence of Death

Integral to Christian vision is the idea of creatures who have such dual membership—who belong to a world of space, time, and bodies, *and* who are made for the God who creates but transcends this finite world. We can never, therefore, say only one thing about our aging and dying. Those events will be as complex as our nature is, and they can always be described from the perspective either of our finitude or our God-directed freedom. The trick is to manage both perspectives simultaneously, distinguishing the two without separating them, holding them together without merging them. Perhaps we can never manage perfectly such a juggling act, but we need to try—to think of human beings both as bodies, for whom the relentless succession of hours and days leads surely to the grave, and as God-aimed spirits, whose every moment is lived in the presence of the Eternal. We are both "out of nature and hopelessly in it."[10] How shall we speak of the aging and dying of such creatures?

We are made for the living God. As the hart longs for cooling streams, so, writes the psalmist, does our soul thirst for God.[11] And, again, if even the sparrow finds a home and the swallow a nest for her young, shall we not long for the courts of the Lord?[12] We are made in God's image to respond to him with the God-breathed spirit that gives life to our finite bodies; and we are called by name in the waters of baptism, in which we are incorporated into the life of the One whom the Father calls his beloved Son.

This is the first and most lasting ground of our individuality and our equality. Before God, who calls us by name, we are singled out as individuals. And whatever the number of our days may thus far have been, we are equidistant from that eternal God. From this perspective death must be seen as profoundly *un*natural. However common it is for human beings to age and die, however regular an occurrence in our experience, death remains an affront to our nature. To be sure, since finite bodies grow older and finally die as time passes, we may call such aging natural; certainly it recurs regularly in our experience. But the "natural" may also signify what is appropriate to a particular being, what constitutes that being's fulfillment and flourishing. In this sense death must be unnatural for those made for fellowship with the One Who Is, those whose full humanity has been revealed in Jesus of Nazareth—who shrank from death and is now the living One.

Death is fearful not only because it means an end to the many experiences we hold dear in this earthly life — though, to be sure, that loss is great. But the God-aimed eternal spirit that is a human being longs for more than a greater quantity of this life. We desire something qualitatively different, "some state . . . toward which our earthly activities are directed but which cannot be attained during earthly life."[13] Because death threatens the loss of that end for which we are created, one of the standard ways of dealing with its terror does not finally persuade. Cicero, for example, in his *De Senectute,* offers this standard argument: If death is the way to a new existence, there is no need to worry. And if, on the other hand, death altogether destroys the soul, there is also no need to worry, since we will no longer exist.[14] But we may want to question at least the second of these claims; for if we no longer exist, our deepest present desire — the longing for God — will have been vain and futile. Desiring such a fulfillment, we will even now be absurd indeed. The threat of death will not give way to such a theory or argument. It gives way, Christians believe, only to an event: the presence of God in the living Jesus.

Hence, it is precisely when we see how much we have to lose in death that we see the fullness of its dread and terror. If we were simply finite beings, interchangeable members of a species that perpetuated itself through our reproduction, death might simply be a component — even a necessary component — of life. But if God has called us by name and called us to himself, if that is our destiny, then in our dying someone unique passes from existence.[15] Thus, Helmut Thielicke writes, "the unnaturalness of death becomes apparent only when we speak of it in connection with God."[16] Simply to describe death as natural, to try to rid it of its ultimate terror by seeing it as part of the rhythm of life, to view it only from the perspective of the finite — this is to risk losing the deepest ground of our individuality and equality.

Having said this, we must not forget, however, that it is also appropriate to think of ourselves as finite beings, limited by biological and historical constraints. As such, we do not live forever; at best we live out what one might term a natural life span. This is not only a matter of years, not only growing old rather than dying while still relatively young. Rather, however difficult it may be to articulate, we tend to think that a "full" life has a certain kind of shape and direction, involves certain stages of development. Nor is this a peculiarly modern insight, for it is common wisdom that Cicero expresses:

> Life's race-course is fixed; Nature has only a single path and that path is run but once, and to each stage of existence has been allotted its own appropriate quality; so that the weakness of childhood, the impetuosity of youth, and the seriousness of middle life, the maturity of old age — each bears some of Nature's fruit, which must be garnered in its own season.[17]

Similarly, Isaiah's vision of the day when the Lord would create new heavens and a new earth, the restoration of life as it should be, makes room for old age as the natural fulfillment of life.

> No more shall there be in [Jerusalem]
>   an infant that lives but a few days,
>   or an old man who does not fill out his days....[18]

What would it mean to have filled out one's days, to have completed the race course of life? It turns out that a "natural" life span is not an easy thing to specify. Cicero suggests that "satiety" is the key. There comes a time when one is satiated with life, and at that point death is the natural culmination of life. Thus, Cicero says, little children enjoy certain activities; eventually, however, they have their fill of these pursuits and move on to youth. That stage too has its characteristic pursuits, and sooner or later we have enough of them and pass on to adulthood. Even there, however, satiety eventually occurs, and we move gradually into old age. It is not simply a time of quiescence; like every other stage of life it has its characteristic activities and concerns. But eventually we become satiated with them, "and when that happens man has his fill of life and the

time is ripe for him to go."[19] Considering the biblical
notion of dying "full of years," Stephen Sapp has made
a rather similar suggestion. For a person to be full of
years, he writes, is somewhat like a vessel being filled
to capacity. "It can hold no more and has fulfilled its
purpose by containing all that it was designed to hold."
To live beyond such a fulfillment, beyond the time when
one was "full of years," would be pointless.[20] This is
not unlike one of the elements Daniel Callahan includes
in the meaning of a "tolerable death": that one's life
possibilities have on the whole been accomplished.[21]

These rather similar suggestions are not free of problems. We might, in the first place, worry about the
"flavor" of these proposals, their hint that the productive, independent life is the truly worthwhile one. While
it is true that our actions over time tend to carve out
for us a kind of individuality—an identity which makes
us more than just interchangeable members of the species—we can see here the limits to such individuality.
It does not reach quite deep enough to capture the
individual worth of one who can do little or nothing,
but whom God still knows by name. We might also, in
the second place, ponder the implications of the notion
of satiety. The idea that life might at some point lose
its ability to charm and interest us suggests that the
natural world—which, theologically, we must call the
creation—might finally fail us. In one sense—but in a
sense that applies to every moment of life and not just
to old age—this is clearly true. I noted above that for
Christian vision this world cannot bear the whole
weight of the heart's longing, since in loving God we
desire not simply more of this life, but something qualitatively different. Nevertheless, this world through
which we make our way to God remains his good gift
to us. And part of the meaning of the deadly sin of
"sloth" is precisely that we might fail the creation—
which is far more likely than that it should fail us. That
we might one day fail to discern the beauty of the rising

sun or the tranquillity of twilight. That we might lose the capacity to delight in a child's first steps or the passion and power of love. If I tire of reading *Goodnight Moon* to a child — as no child will tire of hearing it read — has something in the creation failed me, or have I failed it? It is true that we may, as we grow older, become satiated with life. But perhaps that can be failure — even moral and spiritual failure — on our part.

There remains still a third difficulty with the notion of satiety as an explanation of a full life. Whatever the precise details, versions of the satiety argument seek some kind of natural limit to life other than simply the wearing down of our finite body, our biological self. We can think of obvious candidates for such a natural limit: Time to see our children grown and our grandchildren born. Time to complete important projects in life, to fulfill the obligations and commitments to others that we have undertaken. But Leon Kass is correct, I think, to argue that such approaches will not work. They suggest — and, indeed, are precisely intended to suggest — that we might have filled out our days and be ready to die even if we remained in the best of health. Kass notes quite rightly, however, that death might then seem even more objectionable — taking one still vigorous and still quite capable of the very activities that make life full.[22] The concept of a natural life span needs, finally, a grounding in our biological nature, not just in our history. "Withering is nature's preparation for death. . . ."[23] We need withering and senescence lest we deceive ourselves into imagining that everything we desire could be given through more of the same kind of life. Otherwise we may seek "an endless present, isolated from anything truly eternal."[24] And, one might add, we need withering if we are to cultivate within ourselves the deepest rhythm of love — the mystery of self-giving and self-sacrifice that is God's love. For in growing old we make place for those who come after us. That is biological fact, but we make it an act of love when we understand and accept that, in Kass's words, "if they are truly to flower, we must go to seed; we must wither and give ground" in which they can take root.[25]

To discern the necessity of death in our finitude, in the simple biological truth that we wear out, has a great deal of appeal, and it helps us to understand why we react quite differently to the "premature" death of a young boy than to the death of an elderly man "full of years." Cicero's metaphor nicely captures at least something of what we feel.

> [W]hatever befalls in accordance with Nature should be accounted good; and indeed, what is more consonant with Nature than for the old to die? But the same fate befalls the young, though Nature in their case struggles and rebels. Therefore, when the young die I am reminded of a strong flame extinguished by a torrent; but when old men die it is as if a fire had gone out without the use of force and of its own accord, after the fuel had been consumed. . . . [26]

This image, of fuel having been consumed, is, for me at least, more attractive and less worrisome than the image of a container filled to capacity. In a finely wrought essay, Lewis Thomas has developed a rather similar image.[27] Relying on a poem by Oliver Wendell Holmes about a carriage made by a deacon, Thomas tries to distinguish between a life that *breaks down* and (what would be for him a truly natural culmination) a life that *wears out.* The deacon fashioned his carriage with such care that it was the "perfect organism" — each part as good as all the rest, with no weak link. Had there been a weak link, and had that link broken down, the carriage might have halted prematurely, before its time. But instead, since it never breaks down, the whole gradually wears out. As the poem puts it: "A general flavor of mild decay,/But nothing local, as one may say." And finally, one day it simply goes to

pieces: "All at once, and nothing first." This is Thomas's
picture of a good natural death. When and if we reach
the point where disease does not take us prematurely,
when there is nothing that causes us to break down,
our bodies can simply wear out. In Kass's word, we
"wither."

How does Thomas respond to the thought of such a
death? "No tears, no complaints, no listening closely
for last words. No grief. Just, in the way of the world,
total fulfillment." Perhaps. But perhaps we ought to
wonder just a bit. *Total* fulfillment? Thomas does add
the qualifier, "in the way of the world." Still, the way
of our world, of creatures marked by the duality that
marks us, cannot be captured solely in terms of our
finitude. Such a death, and such an evaluation of it,
suggests a vision that asks too little, that chokes off
the heart's longing for God. Much in it is appealing,
but it cannot comprehend everything we need to say.

We are bodies, aging in time. We are spirits made
for One who exists beyond time. And in thinking about
our living and our dying we must somehow see and
think both truths about ourselves, we must distinguish
but not separate these two perspectives on human nature. One way to avoid such separation is to note that
each angle of vision may shed light upon the other. We
may appreciate our world for what it is only when we
also see—from the perspective of the Eternal—what
it is not and cannot naturally become. And we may see
better how to live before and toward God only as we
remember that the way to God must be traversed, lived
out in this world, where, amidst much sorrow and suffering, there is also much in which to take joy. Below
I offer three brief illustrations of ways in which the
two angles of vision can interact, enriching and qual-
ifying one another in our thinking. The first is an example from the realm of medical care, an inquiry into
the meaning of proper care for the dying. The second
also deals with medical treatment, but takes up what

is best described as a question of public policy, the issue of rationing care for the elderly. And the third turns away from larger questions about our obligations to others in order to think about how we ought to live toward death.

III. Christian Vision Applied

The task of caring for the dying has been greatly complicated by medical advances of recent decades; yet its deepest difficulties are more fundamental still. Chapter 3 of Paul Ramsey's *The Patient as Person* — a chapter titled "On (Only) Caring for the Dying" — remains a classic Christian treatment of the meaning of care.[28] Ramsey argues that we care properly for the dying when we acknowledge that at some point their death is irretrievably upon them and should no longer be resisted, but he also argues that "care" can never include actions intended to cause death. Put very simply: although we should never aim to kill, we can and should sometimes allow to die. We should "never abandon care" — and such abandonment can come either through hastening death, or through struggling vainly against death when its time has come, a struggle that will deflect us from giving the care really needed at that point.

Ramsey recognizes, however, that from two different viewpoints — diametrically opposed, yet strangely similar — one might object to this distinction between killing and allowing to die.[29] Some might claim that whether we kill or allow to die the result is the same: death. Hence, these opponents conclude, we should never give up the struggle against death. We should not intend to kill; neither should we allow to die. We should simply fight death until the matter is taken out of our hands. Other opponents begin from the same premise: that whether we aim to kill or allow to die, what counts morally is that the same result — death — follows. Hence, *they* conclude, we should not only allow to die but also, on some occasions, deliberately kill (in order, for example, to relieve suffering). The first of these opposing views sees human beings as all finitude, needing simply more days and hours, never free to determine that a greater length of days is not the fulfillment for which we are made. The second sees human beings as all freedom — creatures who may seek to master even death, since it does not confront us with the limit that is God.

Ramsey's approach, by contrast, grounded in the paradoxical duality of our nature as finite *and* free, must seek to balance the intricate simultaneities to which this duality gives rise. Hence, a policy of always caring, but only caring, for the dying. Grounded in an understanding of human beings in relation to God, this policy may turn out to contain a good bit of humane wisdom. Faith seeks understanding — and sometimes finds it. The true meaning of death appears when we see it as unnatural — not only the loss of all that we love in this earthly life, but also the apparent loss of the One for whom we are created and toward whom we live. Hence, death is an evil, not to be sought. And yet, more days and years, more of the same, is also not the good our hearts desire — and, hence, we need not cling to this life as if it were our god. Faith makes a double movement — treasuring life as good, but not the highest good; resisting death as evil, even though not the greatest evil. And still more, faith — looking at death through the prism of the crucified and risen Jesus — trusts that this evil can be used for good, that the boundary of death will prove to be not the negation but the fulfillment of our pilgrimage.[30]

Hence, death should always be mourned; sorrow is always fitting even when death is acknowledged, even when faith describes it in the language of fulfillment. Whether death comes upon us in youth or old age, suddenly or after prolonged illness or decline, one whom God called by name is gone. From the vantage point of that relation to God our true individuality apears, and we see the loss death brings. Indeed, we may not cherish each other's body and life as we ought unless we discern in one another the image of the God who calls us to himself. If I too readily accept your dying, if I think of it simply as part of the natural rhythm of life, I may value your person too little.

Not only our individuality but also our equality is most firmly grounded in the God-relation. We can see this if we turn from thinking about care for a particular person to a problem for public policy. Consider, for example, a choice between two kinds of rationing schemes described by Norman Daniels.[31] Faced with limited medical resources we might use an age criterion to distribute those resources. That is, we could say that those who had lived beyond a "normal life span" (perhaps age seventy-five) would not be eligible to receive a variety of life-extending but very costly medical treatments (for example, transplant surgery). These treatments could be developed and used, but their use would be restricted to those who had not yet lived out that normal span of life. An alternative scheme might be a kind of lottery—in which sophisticated and expensive technologies that could not be available for all were allocated by random. In this case, of course, a very old woman might receive the treatment—say, kidney dialysis—that could otherwise have saved a young child.

Daniels, whose aim is to develop a "prudential life span" theory of distributing medical resources, believes that the first approach—the age criterion—is preferable. Since all of us are first young and then older, he suggests that such an approach would treat no one unfairly. Therapies available to all of us when we were young would be available to none of us once we grew sufficiently old. This is a policy, we might say, that tries to take seriously the shape of our finite life. It reckons with the fact that there is a measure to our days and a patterned form to human life. And it seeks to treat us equally over the course of a whole life, even if not at every moment of that life. Still, such an approach to distributive justice may trouble us. It does so in part because it grounds purpose and meaning—as well as fairness—in the shape of a whole life and not also in every moment of it. If this policy tries to treat us equally by remembering that we each live out the life span, it still invites us to treat some of our days and years as if they counted for less than others, as if each moment were not lived before God. And a society in which each of us is invited to treat our years of decline as less valuable than our more vigorous, productive years may find it difficult to get away from the comparative judgments *between* human beings that Daniels himself is eager to avoid. It may prove to be a society inhospitable to the nonproductive and the dependent. I do not argue that this must happen—only that we are not foolish to wonder if it might. A vision which sees every moment of life as equidistant from the Eternal may better preserve our equal worth.

Indeed, I am inclined to think that Daniels's proposal would be safe only in a society that thought of human life not simply in terms of a normal life span but also as directed toward God. We can see how this might be true if we consider an argument about capital punishment made by Camus.[32] He suggested that the justice or injustice of the death penalty depended on the ultimate frame of reference within which it was used and understood. And he argued that capital punishment could be justified only where there was a socially shared religious belief that the final verdict on any person's life was not given in this world. In such a religious society, to condemn a fellow human being to death would not involve divine pretension.[33] Those who issued and executed the verdict would know that, however necessary it seemed to be, it could still be overturned by the only perfectly competent judge, God himself. But what of a society that lacked such beliefs? In it, Camus thought, execution would mean elimination from the only human community that indisputably existed; and, hence, execution would be a godlike activity. Only in a society that believed in the Eternal could it be right to act as if this finite life were not everything.

Similarly, one might decide that an account of justice grounded in a notion of a normal life span — grounded, that is, in the developed form of a life that includes infancy, youth, adulthood, and old age — might be safest in a society of people who did not believe that this was the only truth about our nature. It is one thing to put forward a vision of the limits of this finite life if we believe that our lives are also touched by and directed toward the infinite God. It is quite another to claim a comprehensive vision and mastery of this life — our own and that of others — when we acknowledge nothing more. We know best how to oppose and how to acknowledge death when we do not think of it simply as natural.

Finally, it may be useful to ponder whether thinking about death from the perspective of our nature as finite and free can give us guidance about how we ought to live as we grow older. Suppose we envision two retirement dinners, honoring two men who have been productive and successful in their work, whose careers have been marked by considerable achievement. At the dinner in honor of the first, the retiree is asked to say a few words near the end of the festivities. He does so with the grace one might have expected and speaks of his hopes and plans for the coming years. He hopes, he says, to keep his hand in with the company, doing some consulting on a limited basis. But he intends also to attempt a little independent entrepreneurial activity, since he has always wanted to publish a newsletter aimed at those who can profit from his experience. He plans some traveling but has in mind also new activities. For example, he has always wanted to learn scuba diving, and now he will have time for it. Finally, he never felt he had sufficient time for community affairs; now, though, he hopes to become active in local politics, perhaps even to run for office.

At the dinner honoring the second retiree, he too is invited to say a few words to those present. He does so, telling his friends and acquaintances how he plans to alter abruptly his life's course. He has one simple plan for the coming years: he wants to learn how to die. To that end, he wants fewer possessions; for, as Cicero put it, "can anything be more absurd in the traveller than to increase his luggage as he nears his journey's end?"[34] He has, he says, much reading that he needs to do. He hopes to write some reminiscenses for his children. And he wants to learn the art of contemplative and intercessory prayer. He intends to begin every day with these words from a prayer by John Baillie:

> Forbid, O Lord God, that my thoughts to-day should be wholly occupied with the world's passing show. Seeing that in Thy lovingkindness Thou hast given me the power to lift my mind to the contemplation of things unseen and eternal, forbid that I should remain content with the things of sense and time. Grant rather that each day may do something so to strengthen my hold upon the unseen world, so to increase my sense of its reality, and so to attach my heart to its holy interests that, as the end of my earthly life draws ever nearer, I may not grow to be a part of these fleeting earthly surroundings, but rather grow more and more conformed to the life of the world to come.[35]

If we were present at these dinners, how would we react? Probably the second talk would be more likely to disconcert the crowd; certainly many would be baffled by it. I confess, however, to finding it more satisfying. Were I in need of important advice, I would sooner approach the second man than the first. Yet, perhaps neither plan for retirement is completely adequate. A kind of fear is concealed in the first man's planned frenzy of activity—fear that he might die with some desire unsatisfied. And so he grabs for as much finitude as he can get. That rush of activity chokes off—or, perhaps conceals and pacifies—the restless heart that wants something quite different from "more of the same."

But even though I have confessed my admiration for the second man, perhaps he too has not managed perfectly the simultaneities required by the duality of our nature. His plans may call to mind the "satiety" image of a full life; for we are not certain how best to describe his intentions. Is he turning from a life of which he has had his fill and is now tired? Or is he, noting that he is wearing out, simply gazing more steadfastly at the One from whom the delights of this life come? Is he tired of drinking from the waters that have sustained his life? Or is he seeking the underground source of those refreshing waters? Whatever we say in answer to such questions, this man's fundamental task in life has not really abruptly changed: he must still live *within* the finite world *before* the eternal God. And he takes the measure of his days best when he uses a significant turning point simply as an occasion to rethink now in the present the significance of what has always been true: that we live every moment of life equidistant from eternity; that, nonetheless, we must walk—moment by moment—the pilgrim's way toward God, and that, always, we must struggle to find a way to do both.

9. The Taste for the Other

Naught's had, all's spent,
Where our desire is got without content.
Shakespeare, *Macbeth*

"In moral enquiry we are always concerned with the question: what *type* of enacted narrative would be the embodiment, in the actions and transactions of actual social life, of this particular theory? For until we have answered this question about a moral theory we do not know what that theory in fact amounts to; we do not as yet understand it adequately."[1] If we take to heart this statement by Alasdair MacIntyre, we will believe that it is one thing to analyze the central themes of Christian ethics and quite another to capture some of the embodied "flavor" of Christian life. Yet, one who has faith and seeks to be faithful is probably better prepared for the rigors of Christian living than is one who has simply learned how to think about moral questions. The life of every believer is, finally, something more than a bundle of moral issues. It is the story of one who is separated by sin from the God for whom we are made and the story of return to that God who has come to us in Jesus. We need, therefore, a paradigmatic story — one that will embody some of the flavor and feel of Christian existence.

Perhaps the most powerful of all such stories is the one St. Augustine tells in his *Confessions*. And since, as we noted earlier, Augustine lived in cultural circumstances much like ours, his may be an especially helpful story from which to learn. In it we hear the authentic voice of one struggling to be faithful in the journey back to God, and we get a little of the flavor of such faithfulness — the incompleteness of earthly life, its ordering toward fulfillment in loving union with God, the need for submission to a God who knows us better than we know ourselves, a recognition that the chief barrier to our own happiness lies within us and can be overcome only by God, an understanding that life is inherently social and that we are therefore vulnerable.

The best way to appreciate the paradigmatic force of Augustine's story may be to set it over against a quite different though equally paradigmatic story. And one is readily available, one that may well have been written precisely to offer a contrasting paradigm — namely, the *Confessions* of Jean-Jacques Rousseau. Though often couched in the language of religious piety, Rousseau's story offers a very different vision of human life — the possibility of fulfillment and completion in a moment of earthly history, an insistence on autonomy and independence, a claim that the chief barriers to our happiness lie outside us, a vision of an individual whose happiness lies ultimately in communion with himself. By contrasting these two stories we may taste the distinctive flavor of Christian existence.[2]

Rousseau wants to be independent, even godlike. It is true, of course, that he also wants to "belong," that he desires an unmediated intimacy with others. But he is not willing to accept any belonging that is not the product of his own autonomous will. He wants to submit, desires the pleasures of submission, but is unwilling to submit. Most fundamentally he wills to be his own creator — as he himself makes clear when telling his story.

Some of the happiest times of his early years are spent walking — usually by himself — across the landscape of Europe, and he is a great lover of nature. But nature is not in any sense his instructor or guide; it does not point beyond itself. What the natural world provides is a backdrop—magnificent, to be sure—against which Rousseau, through the creative power of the imagination, constructs an even better world. "For it is impossible for men, and difficult for Nature herself, to surpass the riches of my imagination" (p. 155). How important this is, how closely related to Rousseau's emphasis on independence, becomes clear when he describes the effect nature has on him.

> The sight of the countryside, the succession of pleasant views, the open air, a sound appetite, and the good health I gain by walking, the easy atmosphere of an inn, the absence of everything that makes me feel my dependence, of everything that recalls me to my situation—all these serve to free my spirit, to lend a greater boldness to my thinking, to throw me, so to speak, into the vastness of things, so that I can combine them, select them, and make them mine as I will, without fear or restraint. I dispose of all Nature as its master. (p.158)

We get here some sense of what Rousseau means when he says that he has never been more himself than in his journeys alone and on foot (p.157). With no other human face to call him out of himself, no "other" to question his mastery of all he surveys or require of him even the preliminary act of submission that recognition of otherness entails, he could be freely himself.

Exactly the same desire for independent mastery is displayed in Rousseau's relationships with women. Longing for love, driven in fact by masochistic yearnings to submit, he nevertheless cannot be happy with any woman who is not his own creation. Describing the heat of passion in which he began to compose his novel *La nouvelle Heloise*, Rousseau writes:

> The impossibility of attaining the real persons precipitated me into the land of chimeras; and seeing nothing

that existed worthy of my exalted feelings, I fostered them
in an ideal world which my creative imagination soon peo-
pled with beings after my own heart.... Altogether ignoring the human race, I created for myself societies of
perfect creatures ... such as I had never found here below.
(p. 398)

This is analogous to the manner in which, in his *Emile*,
Rousseau has the tutor introduce Emile to "woman."
The tutor has raised Emile entirely free of corrupting
social influences, but he cannot forever live alone. When
the time comes, therefore, that the young man must
learn to live in society, the tutor introduces him first
into the smallest of societies — the family. He develops
in Emile an inclination to live in society by introducing
him to woman. But he does this first through conversation. He and Emile talk, they develop a picture of the
ideal woman for whom they must seek. The creative
imagination comes first. Only then do they look for
someone who can measure up to the ideal they have
constructed.

Love requires fidelity and submission to another person, but Rousseau seeks independence and mastery.
Hence, his persistent attraction, as he confesses at several places, to the vice of masturbation, "that dangerous means of cheating Nature" (p. 108). What is its
attraction for Rousseau? Quite simply that it obviates
the need for genuine encounter with one who is other
than the self. "This vice, which shame and timidity find
so convenient, has a particular attraction for lively
imaginations. It allows them to dispose, so to speak,
of the whole female sex at their will, and to make any
beauty who tempts them serve their pleasure without
the need of first obtaining her consent" (p. 109). The
aim is for autonomy and mastery.

By contrast, the central theme of Augustine's story,
memorably articulated at its outset, is the desire for a
good outside the self: "You have made us for yourself,
and our hearts are restless until they can find peace

in you" (I, 1). Augustine struggles against God, he seeks
satisfaction in many other goods (sensual pleasure, philosophy, public honor), but from the beginning he is
seeking a fulfillment that lies outside himself. To be
sure, that is not the goal of his undivided self; his being
is not whole. Just as Rousseau, struggling for autonomy,
also desires intimacy and the pleasures of submission,
even so Augustine, wanting to "get in" and belong, still
fights against the need to give himself in trust. But
that struggle for independence he eventually learns to
call sin. He is moved by the story of Victorinus, a pagan
philosopher whose statue was set up in the Roman
forum, but who became a Christian when the day came
that "he did not blush to become the child of your
Christ, an infant at your font, bending his neck to the
yoke of humility and submitting his forehead to the
ignominy of the Cross" (VIII, 2).[3] And, writes Augustine, "I was on fire to be like him, . . . but I was held
back" (VIII, 2). In order to overcome his own desire for
independence and follow the example of Victorinus, Augustine must overcome the division within his will. For
Rousseau the problem is always external to the self in
social circumstances that alienate him from himself,
and the solution is either complete withdrawal from
society or a revolutionary reconstruction of society so
that one can live in community without needing to submit to any other person. For Augustine, however, the
problem is not external. "I was held back not by fetters
put on me by someone else, but by the iron bondage
of my own will" (VIII, 6).

Augustine had not always analyzed his weakness in
this way. As a Manichaean for more than a decade,
Augustine had been attracted to an account far more
like that given by Rousseau. In the dualistic cosmology
of the Manichees the power of good is limited by an
equally sovereign power of evil, and the self is caught
within the struggle between these powers — a struggle,
therefore, external to itself. Moreover, as Peter Brown

notes, for the Manichees the power of goodness had a certain passive quality. The powers of darkness invade the domain of goodness; the genuine self is trapped within the realm of evil. "Their religion was directed to ensuring that this, the good part of themselves, would remain essentially untouched and unaffected by their baser nature."[4] Or, as Augustine himself describes the comforting result of such a cosmology, "they preferred to believe that your substance could suffer evil rather than that their substance could do evil" (VII, 3).

Indeed, so persuaded is Augustine that our predicament lies within ourselves that, in order to be true to this insight, he will risk reversing the Manichaean claim. In order to assert the ontological priority of goodness, he will (in theory, though hardly in his experience) make evil strangely passive. This is the effect of his privative theory of evil by means of which he broke free intellectually from the Manichaean system. If good and evil are not equal, independent powers mutually limiting one another, if goodness has ontological priority, then all evil is only a lack or privation or corruption of what is good. Evil has no positive existence. We may put his point this way: Only the Good is truly creative. The most Evil can do is pervert or corrupt what is good, but it cannot create a single good thing. It can mimic the good, but no more than that; for even the devil is a fallen angel. And when we are drawn to evil, it is because we love a good thing in the wrong way. The problem and predicament lie not in the things we love but in the self who does the loving.

"It was I who willed it, and it was I who was unwilling. It was the same 'I' throughout. But neither my will nor my unwillingness was whole and entire" (VIII, 10). The controversy Augustine describes is "in my heart — about self, and self against self" (VIII, 11) — but not resolved by self. He needed the one thing he had not found in the books of the Platonists: "the face and look of pity, the tears of confession, your *sacrifice*" (VII,

21). And he is given that when in the garden he hears the child's voice directing him, as he concludes, to seek an oracle from the Scriptures; finding it, his heart is "filled with a light of confidence" (VIII, 12).

This is the story Augustine tells, and we do not want to lose sight of how different it is from Rousseau's — how different from the very outset. For, if Augustine has not always known the object of his desire, he has always believed that his happiness lay outside himself. His aim has not, therefore, been to master the world or assert his independence, but to find within it someone or something that could bear the whole weight of the heart's longing. However reluctant he has been to submit, he has in fact always been turned in the direction of such submission. How different an orientation this is from Rousseau's can be seen if we consider Augustine's response to the natural world and compare it with Rousseau's.[5]

In some respects Augustine may seem far less interested than Rousseau in nature. Augustine's focus is so relentlessly on the self that the natural world seems to claim relatively little attention. Thus, for example, in his famous discussion of memory Augustine marvels at the fact that the human mind is too large to understand itself, and he writes:

> At this thought great wonder comes over me; I am struck dumb with astonishment. And men go abroad to wonder at the heights of mountains, the huge waves of the sea, the broad streams of rivers, the vastness of the ocean, the turnings of the stars — and they do not notice themselves. . . . (X, 8)

Yet, in fact, the natural world does have, for Augustine, its own beauty and worth. It is not simply a backdrop that sets free the creative imagination, as it is for Rousseau. Instead, it is a pointer. In and through the natural world we are directed toward the Creator. Hence, nature is to be appreciated, but only as part of the self's movement toward God.

And what is this God? I asked the earth and it answered: "I am not he," and all things that are on the earth
confessed the same answer. I asked the sea and the deeps
and the creeping things with living souls, and they replied,
"We are not your God. Look above us." I asked the blowing
breezes, and the universal air with all its inhabitants answered: "Anaximenes was wrong. I am not God." I asked
the heaven, the sun, the moon, the stars, and "No," they
said, "we are not the God for whom you are looking." And
I said to all those things which stand about the gates of
my senses: "Tell me something about my God, you who
are not He. Tell me something about Him." And they cried
out in a loud voice: "He made us." (X, 6)

Here the creation, though clearly desacralized, bears
witness and points beyond itself to the God from whom
all living things come. This is strikingly different from
Rousseau's manner of reveling in nature as a backdrop
against which to feel his own existence. Nature could
not give Rousseau what he desires were it constantly
pointing him beyond himself, reminding him of his dependence on God. Its beauty for him is that—unlike
the company of other human beings—it makes no demands, holds no one accountable.

Augustine's approach is not without its dangers. He
may seem to reduce the significance of every created
good to the status simply of "pointer toward God."
Having let God into his life, having realized that his
happiness can be found only in God, he has let in the
incalculable—and he may seem to have made the world
a less enchanting place. This does not, however, actually
seem to happen with respect to the world of nature.
Perhaps surprisingly, a nature that points beyond itself
to God turns out to be more mysterious than nature
was for Rousseau, the great romantic. Just as Rousseau
claims to know himself, to know his heart, so he also
thinks he can comprehend nature. During his short stay
on St. Peter's Island, a stay devoted in large measure
to "botanizing," he intended to describe "all the plants

of the island, without omitting a single one, in sufficient detail to occupy myself for the rest of my days."[6] Given sufficient time, the human mind could encompass and categorize the world of nature — or so Rousseau thought. Not so Augustine. As the self is for him a mystery, so is nature. Indeed, in order to describe the unknowability of the self, Augustine has recourse to metaphors from the natural world. "What then am I, my God? What is my nature? A life various, manifold, and quite immeasurable. Imagine the plains, caverns, and abysses of my memory; they are innumerable . . ." (X, 17). To be sure, Augustine is confident that nature can be known in part.[7] And why not, since it receives its order from God? A world that points beyond itself to God must be in some sense an understandable world; otherwise we could never receive its message. But it must also be an ultimately mysterious and unfathomable world; for it finds its meaning in the vastness of an infinite light.

Augustine is not always as successful in managing the dualities of loving another person or thing "in God." To be on the way toward that incalculable God can threaten all other loves. Once the "pointer" has done its work and directed us beyond itself to its Maker, why should we any longer pay it heed? We can see the problem exemplified in Augustine's examination in Book X of the temptations to which he may still be subject along his pilgrim way. He considers temptations incited by our sense of taste — and he worries, then, about his love for food. Worrying about it, he formulates what we might call a theory of "food as medicine," food as something to be used but not exactly enjoyed.

> This you have taught me, that I should have the same attitude toward taking food as I have toward taking medicine. But while I pass from the discomfort of hunger to the satisfaction of sufficiency, in that very moment of transition there is set for me a snare of concupiscence. For the moment of transition is pleasurable, and we are forced

to go through that moment; there is no other way. And while we eat and drink for the sake of health, there is a dangerous kind of pleasure which follows in attendance on health and very often tries to put itself first. . . . (X, 31)

The point of food, as Augustine describes it here, is only that it preserves us during our pilgrimage toward God. No doubt this is not the most important example, but Augustine adopts a parallel attitude toward sexuality. Indeed, in quite different ways both Augustine and Rousseau have difficulty attaching themselves to a flesh-and-blood woman. Rousseau cannot, since such attachment seems to require submission. He must therefore prefer the woman furnished by his creative imagination, one whom he can make serve his pleasure "without the need of first obtaining her consent." Augustine, by contrast, seems to feel that in order to journey toward God he must tear himself free from love of woman. "The woman with whom I was in the habit of sleeping was torn from my side on the grounds of being an impediment to my marriage, and my heart, which clung to her, was broken and wounded and dropping blood" (VI, 15). If the reasons here are complicated by Monica's plans for her son's marriage, it is clear that Augustine later understands his conversion to be incompatible with love of woman.

Thus, he treats the pleasures of sexuality as he does those of food. One ought not seek pleasure in eating, even as one ought not seek the pleasures of sexual companionship. As the purpose of eating is to sustain life, so the purpose of sexuality should be simply preservation of the human species. Food he cannot give up entirely, of course, but sex he can — leaving the task of procreation to those who will also have to suffer its temptations. Augustine has often been faulted for his attitude on such questions, and no doubt there is room for criticism, but may it not be that we sometimes criticize simply because we have not felt as strongly

as Augustine does the pilgrim character of our life?
That we shrink from considering what it might mean
to place God at the center of all our loves? Writing of
Augustine's "examination of conscience" in Book X,
Robert O'Connell nicely states the criticism:

> That examination of conscience makes, surely, some of
> the most depressing reading in all of Christian literature.
> There is something profoundly saddening about the por-
> trait it presents: the great Bishop of Hippo tormenting
> himself about the pleasure he cannot avoid while eat-
> ing . . . or listening to psalmody . . . ; berating himself that
> the spectacle of a dog chasing a hare, or of a lizard snaring
> a fly, can still distract his interest. . . . Even more sad-
> dening, perhaps, the thought of Christian generations who
> have been confused and troubled by the dreadful indict-
> ment of those wholesome human things, to say nothing of
> Christians today and tomorrow who, influenced by pages
> like these and others following their inspiration, will con-
> tinue to doubt their own healthy acceptance of the world
> God made "good," indeed, "very good."[8]

Perhaps. But I do not have it in me to be saddened.
For Augustine surely knew that all these created things
were good. But he did not, in remembering that, forget
that they were *created* — and that they could not, therefore, bear the whole weight of the heart's longing. He
sought to take them up into a life directed wholly and
entirely toward God. If he did not always manage to
capture adequately the double affirmation required for
such a life, he at least did not let go the sense of being
on the way. He did not forget that his happiness lay in
faithfulness to God, nor did he fail to reckon with how
incalculable were the results of his realization that he
was made for God. He had been grasped by "the face
and look of pity, the tears of confession, your *sacrifice*."
Henceforth, no created thing or person could be God
for him; he could only live out his pilgrimage as faithfully as he was able.

Being free of attachment to a woman is, for Rousseau, simply one important aspect of the freedom he desires — the freedom of an autonomous self-creator. Augustine means something quite different when he writes, "I was still closely bound by my need of woman" (VIII, 1). He can find no way to give himself to God that does not — at least for him — involve tearing his heart free from such need and love. But the crucial point is this: He is seeking to give himself to God — not to be independent, but to acknowledge his need for God. Indeed, this is precisely how he describes that climactic moment in the garden when his heart "was filled with a light of confidence." In that moment, he writes, "you converted me to you in such a way that I no longer sought a wife . . . " (VIII, 12). Renunciation here is for the sake of enjoyment. Freedom from the need to submit to a woman is freedom for dependence upon God — a still more absolute Other to whom a greater submission is required. Augustine bypasses one kind of love and dependence, but his aim in so doing is not independence. He simply affirms in his own individual way the truth that our happiness lies outside ourselves, that we are made for God. Believing himself to be always on the way, Augustine finds deliverance in humbling himself before the One who had humbled himself — in "the face and look of pity."

No one should say that Augustine's way, the pilgrim's way, is free of risk. Indeed, what for Augustine brings deliverance and enlargement of being seems to Rousseau to be a kind of annihilation of the self. And certainly, Augustine's vision of human life — though ravishingly alluring in certain moments — is in other ways a very somber one. Robert Meagher has articulated this aspect of Augustine's thought with clarity.[9] For Augustine, genuine happiness requires two things: (1) We must love rightly what is good. This means, most simply, that we cannot rest the whole weight of the heart's longing in any created thing, however good; for only God can satisfy that longing. (2) We must "possess" the good we love. Hence, we cannot take the stoic way, stifle our longing for enjoyment, and imagine that commitment to the good without possession of it is sufficient to satisfy the heart's longing.

The pathos of our life, however, is that—within human history—these two requirements are incompatible. We must choose (1) to love rightly but not possess the good we love—since in this life the heart cannot rest fully in God and we live by faith, not sight. Or we must choose (2) to love a good we can possess—which must mean, however, a good that cannot ultimately satisfy the longing of our pilgrim heart. Augustine, of course, is persuaded that we should make the first of these choices, but he recognizes the terrors of such a choice. "Here I have the power but not the wish to stay; there I wish to be but cannot; both ways miserable" (X, 40).

Despite its somber tone, however, there is in Augustine's view of the self an expansiveness and a richness that we ought not miss. He submits to God but is not stultified by such submission. He admits that he cannot fully know himself, and in this admission he finds enlarged scope for wonder. The reader beginning Augustine's *Confessions* is likely to get the impression that its author thinks he knows the meaning of his life and intends to convey that meaning. Perhaps Augustine himself thought that at the outset. But the attempt to tell the story leads to deeper insight. The inquiring self turns out to be too vast for self-comprehension. "What then am I, my God? What is my nature? A life various, manifold, and quite immeasurable. . . . I dive down deep as I can, and I can find no end" (X, 17). A created self, like any created thing, must finally remain mysterious—knowable in part, but finding its full significance only in God. Having attempted the telling of his story, Augustine is forced to conclude that such a goal is really beyond him. God knows him better than he knows himself. Therefore his autobiography becomes confession—confession of his sin, to be sure, but also confession of the praise of God (X, 2). "So I will confess what I know of myself, and I will also confess what I do not know of myself" (X, 5).

Rousseau, by contrast, recognizes no such limit to his ability to know himself. Nor need he, of course, since he thinks of himself as a self-creator, forged in the fires of his own creative imagination. Thus, the famous claim at the outset of his *Confessions:*

> Let the last trump sound when it will, I shall come forward with this work in my hand, to present myself before my Sovereign Judge, and proclaim aloud: "... I have bared my secret soul as Thou thyself hast seen it, Eternal Being. So let the numberless legion of my fellow men gather round me, and hear my confession. Let them groan at my depravities, and blush for my misdeeds. But let each one of them reveal his heart at the foot of Thy throne with equal sincerity. . . ." (p. 17)

He appeals to sincerity, the cardinal virtue of modernity. How different is this claim from Augustine's, as Robert Meagher characterizes it: "To give an account of one's life, then, is not simply to say 'such was my life' but to confess the faithful or faithless character of that life" to the only One who can see it whole.[10]

Rousseau seeks to be himself. Augustine, able to say only that God knows him better than he knows himself, must direct his attention outside himself: "Let me know you, my knower . . . " (X, 1).[11] And this turn outward is what enriches Augustine's vision; for, consider finally where these two quite different sorts of confession end. Rousseau concludes his story shortly after his eviction from St. Peter's Island. There he thought he had found happiness, a happiness described more fully in the Fifth Promenade of his *Reveries* than in the *Confessions.* He sought, he tells us, a happiness "in no way made up of fleeting instants, but rather a simple and permanent

state."[12] A state, that is, in which we no longer experience any sense of being "on the way," and to which
we could say: *"I would like this instant to last forever."*[13]
Rousseau doubts that we can often find such happiness,
but he knows what he seeks and believes he achieved
it during his short stay on the island. His longest description of such a state of happiness is both powerfully
evocative and instructive:

> But if there is a state in which the soul finds a solid
> enough base to rest itself on entirely and to gather its
> whole being into, without needing to recall the past or
> encroach upon the future; in which time is nothing for it;
> in which the present lasts forever without, however, mak-
> ing its duration noticed and without any trace of time's
> passage; without any other sentiment . . . except that of
> our existence, and having this sentiment alone fill it com-
> pletely; as long as this state lasts, he who finds himself
> in it can call himself happy . . . with a sufficient, perfect,
> and full happiness which leaves the soul no emptiness it
> might feel a need to fill. . . .
>
> What do we enjoy in such a situation? Nothing external
> to ourselves, nothing if not ourselves and our own exis-
> tence. As long as this state lasts, we are sufficient unto
> ourselves, like God.[14]

There Rousseau's journey ends: enclosed within the
narrow confines of an isolated self. The constant struggle to be himself ends with a constricted world—the
self alone with itself. By contrast, how vast is the world
that opens before Augustine when he ceases to worry
about himself and, instead, seeks to learn faithfulness
to God. Is this not the secret to those last books of his
Confessions, books that have puzzled so many interpreters? Augustine writes of time and creation. He
probes the mysteries of the Genesis story of creation.
What, his readers have asked, are such musings doing
in the story of a life? Indeed, interpreters have often
been drawn to versions of the hypothesis that Augustine is simply "clearing his desk," seizing the oppor-

tunity to answer various queries that have been directed to him. "He combines all these parts rather awkwardly, merely placing them in succession one after the other. The result is a badly composed book."[15]

I do not think there is any assured way to disprove such claims; even the evidences of literary connections between the first book and the last can scarcely be determinative.[16] The answer that does persuade me, though, is of a different sort. We must come to care about Augustine's attempt to understand himself as one always "on the way" toward God. That self-understanding transforms his aims, directs his attention to what is outside the self: from the mystery of the single individual—"man who is only a small portion of what you have created" (I, 1)—to the entire creation, all part of a vast movement back to the Creator. "We see the things you have made, because they are, and they are, because you see them" (XIII, 38). Indeed, even at journey's end the pilgrim self is fulfilled only in a life turned toward the Other, steadfastly directed toward God, in whom one can find peace. In that life, Augustine says, "nothing will remain but praise."[17]

Notes

1. The Singularity of Christian Ethics

1. Karl Barth, *Church Dogmatics*, III/2 (Edinburgh: T. & T. Clark, 1957), p. 518.

2. Ibid., p. 519.

3. George A. Lindbeck, *The Nature of Doctrine* (Philadelphia: Westminster Press, 1984), p. 134.

4. Helmut Thielicke, *Theological Ethics*, Volume 1: Foundations (Philadelphia: Fortress Press, 1966), pp. 30-31.

5. St. Augustine, *On Christian Doctrine* (Indianapolis: Bobbs-Merrill, 1958), II, XL, 60.

6. Michael Oakeshott, *Rationalism in Politics and Other Essays* (London: Methuen, 1962), pp. 59-79. Oakeshott's thought is, at its core, Hegelian, and his distinction between two forms of the moral life is clearly a version of Hegel's distinction between *Moralität* and *Sittlichkeit*. References to Oakeshott's essay will be given by page number in parentheses within the body of the text.

7. Alasdair MacIntyre, *After Virtue* (Notre Dame, Ind.: University of Notre Dame Press, 1981), p. 263.

8. Lindbeck, p. 124.

9. Ibid., p. 126.

10. Cf. Richard John Neuhaus, *The Naked Public Square* (Grand Rapids, Mich.: Eerdmans, 1984).

11. Francis Oakley, *The Medieval Experience* (New York: Charles Scribner's Sons, 1974), p. 97f.

12. Lindbeck, p. 118.

13. Cf. Stanley Hauerwas, *Against the Nations* (Minneapolis: Winston Press, 1985), pp. 1-2. Hauerwas suggests, persuasively I think, that an ethic which focuses on the church's

own life flows naturally from Lindbeck's theological program. Hauerwas would not himself employ the term 'sectarian' to describe this approach, but I think the term accurately reflects certain features of his ethic (e.g., an unwillingness to search for continuity between Christian claims and the public order, an interest in exploring the particularity of the Christian life within its narrative context). One might argue that out of Lindbeck's vision an ethic which was Eusebian rather than sectarian might equally well develop. That is, the church might simply attempt to absorb the world—with a vengeance. And, after all, Barth *was* a Calvinist! Nevertheless, relatively few Christian *theologians* today have either the will or the nerve to turn in that direction.

14. Stuart Hampshire, "Morality and Convention," in *Utilitarianism and Beyond*, ed. Amartya Sen and Bernard Williams (Cambridge: Cambridge University Press, 1982), p. 152.

15. The forms of life to which disciples of the later Wittgenstein tend to have recourse seem to be linguistic versions of the modes of experience to which philosophical idealists of an earlier generation had pointed. Within the idealist tradition of thought, however, there was a far greater drive toward unity, which could be balanced against complacent appreciation of the distinctiveness of separate forms of life. The philosophical idealist was more likely to consider whether the separate modes of experience might not be taken up into some greater unity, even if that unity could not always be fully articulated in thought or lived in practice.

16. See, for example, H. L. A. Hart, *The Concept of Law* (Oxford: The Clarendon Press, 1961), p. 181ff.

17. St. Augustine, *City of God*, XII, 22.

18. Josef Pieper, "The Christian West," *Commonweal* 2 (March 15, 1957): 607-9. Citations from Pieper in this and the following paragraph will be from this article.

19. Oakley, p. 204.

20. Josef Pieper, *Scholasticism* (New York: McGraw-Hill, 1964), p. 34.

21. Lindbeck, p. 132.

22. Matthew 6:21.

23. Matthew 12:33ff.

24. William Strunk, Jr., *The Elements of Style*, 3rd ed.,

with Revisions, an Introduction, and a Chapter on Writing by E. B. White (New York: Macmillan, 1979). References will be given by page number in parentheses within the body of the text.

25. Scott Elledge, *E. B. White: A Biography* (New York and London: W. W. Norton, 1984), p. 330.

26. Stanley Hauerwas, *A Community of Character* (Notre Dame, Ind.: University of Notre Dame Press, 1983), p. 221.

27. Philip Abbott, "Philosophers and the Abortion Question," *Political Theory* 6 (August 1978): 329.

28. Paul Ramsey, "Reference Points in Deciding about Abortion," *The Morality of Abortion: Legal and Historical Perspectives*, ed. John T. Noonan, Jr. (Cambridge, Mass.: Harvard University Press, 1970), p. 67.

29. G. K. Chesterton, *The Everlasting Man* (Garden City, N.Y.: Doubleday, 1955), p. 168.

30. Gustaf Wingren, *The Living Word* (Philadelphia: Fortress Press, 1960), p. 192.

31. Helmut Thielicke, *The Evangelical Faith*, Volume 1 (Grand Rapids, Mich.: Eerdmans, 1974). Citations will be given by page number within parentheses in the body of the text.

32. Karl Barth, *Church Dogmatics*, II/2 (Edinburgh: T. & T. Clark, 1957), p. 541.

33. The two ways are distinguished within Galatians but not completely separated. Neither exists in entirely pure form. For example, if we understand *pistis tou huiou tou theou* in 2:20 as a subjective genitive, our understanding of 2:16-21 will be brought closer to the second type of thinking. For then we might say that the only *ergon nomou* that justifies is the faithfulness of Jesus — more a historical than existential emphasis. Moreover, the second way has individualizing elements that lend it a somewhat existential air. Even when Paul discusses the two aeons, he does not speak precisely of being in the new age (but, instead, of being delivered from the present evil age). What is new appears to be confined to those who are under the lordship of Christ. Thus, in 3:26 those who are sons of God through faith are those who are in Christ. And baptism serves as a means for bringing one into Christ (3:27).

34. For this interpretation I am indebted to the first chapter of Harold C. Goddard, *The Meaning of Shakespeare* (Chicago: University of Chicago Press, 1951).

35. *Cymbeline*, III, iii, 89-95.

36. Ibid., 96-98.

37. Charles Norris Cochrane, *Christianity and Classical Culture* (Oxford: Oxford University Press, 1957), p. 318.

38. Ibid., p. 384.

39. R. A. Markus, *Saeculum: History and Society in the Theology of St. Augustine* (Cambridge: Cambridge University Press, 1970), p. 14ff.

40. Cf. Markus, chapter 3.

2. Human Nature: The Human Being

1. Regin Prenter, *Creation and Redemption* (Philadelphia: Fortress Press, 1967), p. 251.

2. George S. Hendry, *Theology of Nature* (Philadelphia: Westminster Press, 1980), p. 17.

3. Cf. H. Paul Santmire, *The Travail of Nature* (Philadelphia: Fortress Press, 1985), p. 130.

4. Cf. Hendry, p. 177. He notes that the very word 'ecology' suggests that the natural world exists to provide an *oikos* for human beings.

5. Owen Barfield, *Saving the Appearances* (New York: Harcourt, Brace & World, 1947), p. 42.

6. Hendry, p. 188.

7. Mary Midgley, *Evolution as a Religion* (London and New York: Methuen, 1985), p. 69.

8. C. S. Lewis, *God in the Dock* (Grand Rapids, Mich.: Eerdmans, 1970), p. 227.

9. Thomas F. Tracy, *God, Action and Embodiment* (Grand Rapids, Mich.: Eerdmans, 1984), p. 57.

10. H. Tristram Engelhardt, Jr., *The Foundations of Bioethics* (New York and Oxford: Oxford University Press, 1986), p. 105.

11. Ibid., p. 129.

12. *Cymbeline*, I, v, 18-24.

13. Engelhardt, p. 117.

14. For this characterization of what it means to be embodied I am indebted to Tracy, p. 110.

15. Helmut Thielicke, *Theological Ethics*, Volume 1: *Foundations* (Philadelphia: Fortress Press, 1966), p. 162.

16. See Oliver O'Donovan, *Begotten or Made?* (Oxford: Clarendon Press, 1984), chapter 4; "Again: Who Is a Person?" pp. 125-37 in *Abortion and the Sanctity of Human Life*, ed. J. H. Channer (Exeter: Paternoster Press, 1986); and *Resurrection and the Moral Order* (Grand Rapids, Mich.: Eerdmans, 1986), 238f.

17. O'Donovan, *Begotten or Made?*, p. 52f.

18. O'Donovan, "Again: Who Is a Person?" p. 129.

19. O'Donovan, *Begotten or Made?*, p. 59.

20. Ibid., p. 59f.

21. William F. May, "Parenting, Bonding, and Valuing the Retarded Child," *Ethics and Mental Retardation*, ed. L. Kopelman and J. C. Moskop (Dordrecht: D. Reidel, 1984), p. 157.

22. I have discussed these questions in somewhat more detail in *Friendship: A Study in Theological Ethics* (Notre Dame, Ind.: University of Notre Dame Press, 1981).

23. John Calvin, *Institutes of the Christian Religion*, Library of Christian Classics, vol. 20, ed. John T. McNeill and trans. Ford Lewis Battles (Philadelphia: Westminster Press, 1960), II, viii, 55 (p. 418f.).

24. Soren Kierkegaard, *Works of Love*, trans. Howard and Edna Hong (New York: Harper Torchbooks, 1964), 156f.

25. See Gene Outka, *Agape: An Ethical Analysis* (New Haven, Conn.: Yale University Press, 1972), 260ff.; and Daniel Day Williams, *The Spirit and the Forms of Love* (New York and Evanston: Harper & Row, 1968), chapter 4.

26. J. L. Stocks, *Morality and Purpose* (New York: Schocken Books, 1969), p. 50.

27. Josef Pieper, *About Love*, trans. Richard and Clara Winston (Chicago: Franciscan Herald Press, 1974), p. 85.

28. Thomas Nagel, *Mortal Questions* (Cambridge: Cambridge University Press, 1979), p. 130.

29. Lewis Hyde, "Some Food We Could Not Eat: Gift Exchange and the Imagination," *The Kenyon Review*, n.s. 1 (Fall 1979): 45.

30. Ibid., p. 53.

31. C. S. Lewis, *Arthurian Torso* (London: Oxford, 1948), p. 123.

3. Human Nature: The Sinful Human Being

1. C. S. Lewis, *Perelandra* (New York: Macmillan, 1944).
2. Ibid., p. 117.
3. Ibid., p. 208.
4. *City of God*, XI, 13.
5. Josef Pieper, *Leisure the Basis of Culture* (New York and Toronto: New American Library, 1963).
6. William F. May, *A Catalogue of Sins* (New York, Chicago and San Francisco: Holt, Rinehart and Winston, 1967), p. 201.
7. C. S. Lewis, *Mere Christianity* (New York: Macmillan, 1960), p. 95.
8. *City of God*, XIV, 11. We will miss the force of the illustration if we focus single-mindedly on Augustine's assumption that Adam was Eve's intellectual superior.
9. Reinhold Niebuhr, *The Nature and Destiny of Man*, Volume 1: *Human Nature* (New York: Charles Scribner's Sons, 1941), p. 269.
10. Ibid., p. 280.
11. Ibid., p. 277.
12. C. S. Lewis, *The Problem of Pain* (New York: Macmillan, 1962), p. 85.
13. G. K. Chesterton, *The Everlasting Man* (Garden City, N.Y.: Doubleday Image Books, 1955), p. 244.
14. Langdon Gilkey, *Maker of Heaven and Earth* (Garden City, N.Y.: Doubleday Anchor, 1965), p. 238.
15. St. Augustine, "On the Grace of Christ and On Original Sin," in *Basic Writings of Saint Augustine*, volume 1, ed. Whitney J. Oates (New York: Random House, 1948), II, xxxiv (p. 643).
16. George Vandervelde, *Original Sin: Two Major Trends in Contemporary Roman Catholic Interpretation* (Washington, D.C.: University Press of America, 1981), p. 331. This is a puzzle for Christian theology, but we need not imagine that it is a silly puzzle. Thus, for example, the philosopher Harry

G. Frankfurt, with no theological ax to grind, speaks of "volitional necessities" which are "both self-imposed and imposed involuntarily." Cf. Frankfurt, *The Importance of What We Care About* (New York: Cambridge University Press, 1988), p. 88. For Frankfurt, such a concept is needed to explain our experience. It is, therefore, strange to find students of religion who seem entirely tone deaf to such possibilities. For example, in *Adam, Eve, and the Serpent* (New York: Random House, 1988) Elaine Pagels depicts St. Augustine as the culprit responsible for a "cataclysmic transformation in Christian thought from an ideology of moral freedom to one of universal corruption" (p. 97). Pagels regularly blurs the distinction between human capacity for choice and the general orientation of the self in service of which all such choices are made. Augustine does not deny—indeed, he affirms— our freedom to make moral choices. But he also holds that all our choices express a self who cannot love God with a whole heart apart from the liberating work of God's own grace. This is Augustine's notion of a "free will in bondage," and it is a notion consistently confused in Pagels's treatment.

17. Lewis, *The Problem of Pain*, p. 86f. (italics added).

18. Austin Farrer, *Love Almighty and Ills Unlimited* (Garden City, N.Y.: Doubleday, 1961), p. 102.

19. *Confessions*, VIII, 5. Cf. Frankfurt, p. 165: "In the absence of wholeheartedness, the person is not merely in conflict with forces 'outside' him; rather, he himself is divided."

4. Human Nature: The Justified Sinner

1. First published in Wittenberg, 1524.

2. Reinhold Niebuhr, *The Nature and Destiny of Man*, Volume II: *Human Destiny* (New York: Charles Scribner's Sons, 1943), p. 104.

3. I have treated these themes elsewhere. See "The Place of Ethics in the Theological Task," pp. 196-203 in *Currents in Theology and Mission* 4 (August 1979); and chapter 5 of *The Theory and Practice of Virtue* (Notre Dame, Ind.: University of Notre Dame Press, 1984).

4. Anders Nygren, *Agape and Eros*, trans. Philip S. Watson (New York and Evanston: Harper & Row, 1969), 83f.

5. That this tension is to some degree permanent may be seen, for example, in the fact that in recent decades, even in a series of dialogues aimed at overcoming theological disagreements, Lutherans and Catholics have recognized that their preferred ways of describing God's justification of the sinner reflect different emphases and concerns. Cf. *Justification by Faith: Lutherans and Catholics in Dialogue* vol. 7, ed. H. George Anderson, T. Austin Murphy, and Joseph A. Burgess (Minneapolis: Augsburg, 1985). Consider just the following two passages:

> Lutherans, primarily intent upon emphasizing God's unconditional saving promises and upon purifying the church from superstition, corruption, and self-glorification, continue to press for a more thoroughgoing application of justification by faith as a critical principle. Catholics, concerned with protecting the fullness of God's gifts as granted through Christ in the Holy Spirit, are on guard against criticism that might erode the catholic heritage. (p. 57)

> The Catholic concerns are most easily expressed in the transformationist language appropriate to describing a process in which human beings, created good but now sinful, are brought to new life through God's infusion of saving grace. . . . Lutheran ways of speaking, on the other hand, are shaped by the situation of sinners standing before God (*coram deo*) and hearing at one and the same time God's words of judgment and forgiveness in law and gospel. (p. 49)

6. *Confessions*, VII, 21.

7. Ibid. X, 36.

8. Ibid. X, 38.

9. Ibid. X, 37.

10. *Luther's Works*, vol. 31 (Philadelphia: Fortress Press, 1957), pp. 329-77.

11. Ibid., p. 358.

12. Ibid., p. 375.

13. Ibid., p. 347.

14. Helmut Thielicke, *Theological Ethics*, vol. 1: *Foundations* (Philadelphia: Fortress Press, 1966), p. 70.

15. Victor Furnish, *Theology and Ethics in Paul* (Nashville and New York: Abingdon, 1968), p. 255.

16. Ernst Käsemann, "God's Righteousness in Paul," *Journal for Theology and the Church*, vol. I, ed. Robert W. Funk, et. al. (New York: Harper & Row, 1965), p. 109.

17. Furnish, p. 215.

18. Ibid., p. 152f.

19. Karl Barth, "Gospel and Law," in *Community, State, and Church* (Gloucester, Mass.: Peter Smith, 1968), p. 78.

20. Niebuhr, *Nature and Destiny . . .* , vol. 2, p. 141.

21. See Romans 5:1, 6:1.

22. That there may be limits to what we should do for the sake of another will be argued in the next chapter. Here my concern is with the peculiarly Christian limits upon what we do for our own sake.

23. Martin Luther, "Temporal Authority: To What Extent It Should Be Obeyed," in *Luther's Works*, vol. 45 (Philadelphia: Muhlenberg Press, 1962), p. 95.

24. Ibid., p. 96.

25. Ibid., p. 104.

26. Ibid.

5. Moral Theory: Rules, Virtues, Results

1. Karl Barth, *Church Dogmatics*, IV/1 (Edinburgh: T. & T. Clark, 1956), p. 448.

2. C. S. Lewis, *Mere Christianity* (New York: Macmillan, 1960), pp. 56f.

3. The language here reflects Thomas Ogletree's *The Use of the Bible in Christian Ethics* (Philadelphia: Fortress Press, 1983).

4. Thomas Nagel, "The Limits of Objectivity," in *The Tanner Lectures on Human Values*, vol. 1, ed. Sterling M. McMurrin (Cambridge: Cambridge University Press, 1980), p. 131.

5. Iris Murdoch, *The Sovereignty of Good* (London: Routledge & Kegan Paul, 1970), p. 80.

6. R. M. Hare, "Moral Conflicts," in *The Tanner Lectures on Human Values*, vol. 1, p. 180.

7. Samuel Scheffler, *The Rejection of Consequentialism* (Oxford: Clarendon Press, 1982), p. 4.

8. Godwin's *An Enquiry Concerning Political Justice and Its Influence on General Virtue and Happiness* was first published in 1793. My citations will come from volume 1 of the edition abridged and edited by Raymond A. Preston (New York: Alfred A. Knopf, 1926). In later editions Godwin modified some of his stands, but Preston's abridgment uses the first edition, in which Godwin sets forth his position most provocatively. Page numbers of citations will be given in parentheses within the body of the text.

9. For example, neither Scheffler nor Nagel is particularly puzzled by the notion that we need not always do what is for the best; they find quite understandable an agent's prerogative to pursue (some of the time) his own projects rather than the general good. (But, then, they are not working within a tradition that has too often had to reckon with practitioners of a Franciscan love.) Such an agent's prerogative is for them reasonably grounded in personal autonomy or the need for personal independence. (In an earlier chapter I have come to a similar conclusion, but on different grounds. Neighbor-love, I suggested, can be self-referential, because a world in which no one had personal desires or projects would be a world in which we could not give ourselves in love to the service of others. It would not be a world of finite creatures with the wide variety of loves implanted in us by our Creator.) Both philosophers, however, are puzzled by the idea that we might sometimes be prohibited from seeking the best outcome even if we wanted to. Even Nagel, who does argue in favor of such a restriction on our freedom to seek what is best, grants that it may seem "primitive, even superstitious" (p. 131). The burden of this chapter is to replace 'superstitious' with 'religious'!

10. John Finnis, *Fundamentals of Ethics* (Washington, D.C.: Georgetown University Press, 1983), p. 93.

11. Henry Sidgwick, *The Methods of Ethics*, Reprint of 7th ed. (Indianapolis and Cambridge: Hackett Publishing Company, 1981), p. 87.

12. Godwin, p. 44.

13. Sidgwick, p. 434.

14. A point made repeatedly by Bernard Williams. For example: "It is artificial to suppose that a thorough commitment to the values of friendship and so on can merely alternate, on a timetable prescribed by calm or activity, with an alien set of reflections. Moreover, since the reflections are indeed alien, some kind of willed forgetting is needed, an internal surrogate of those class barriers on which Sidgwick relied, to keep the committed dispositions from being unnerved by instrumental reflection when they are under pressure." *Ethics and the Limits of Philosophy* (Cambridge, Mass.: Harvard University Press, 1985), p. 109.

15. Michael Stocker, 'The Schizophrenia of Modern Ethical Theories," *Journal of Philosophy* 73 (August 12, 1976): 466.

16. Einar Billing, *Our Calling*, trans. Conrad Bergendorff (Philadelphia: Fortress Press, 1964), p. 17.

17. Charles Dickens, *Christmas Books* (London and Glasgow: Collins, 1954), p. 24.

18. John Henry Cardinal Newman, *Apologia Pro Vita Sua*, edited with an introduction and notes by A. Dwight Culler (Boston: Houghton Mifflin, 1956), p. 234.

19. Shusaku Endo, *Silence*, trans. William Johnston (New York: Taplinger, 1980), p. 259.

20. See D. M. Mackinnon, *A Study in Ethical Theory* (London: Adam & Charles Black, 1957), pp. 97f.

21. Cf. Nagel, p. 132, and Charles Fried, *Right and Wrong* (Cambridge, Mass.: Harvard University Press, 1978), p. 27.

22. Helmut Thielicke, *Theological Ethics*, vol. 1: *Foundations* (Philadelphia: Fortress Press, 1966), p. 614.

23. Michael Walzer, *Just and Unjust Wars* (New York: Basic Books, 1977), see esp. pp. 251-68, 323-27.

24. Cf. Finnis, p. 83.

25. *City of God*, XIX, 6.

26. Thielicke, p. 658.

27. Fried, p. 10.

28. See J. B. Schneewind, *Sidgwick's Ethics and Victorian Moral Philosophy* (Oxford: Clarendon Press, 1977), p. 114.

29. Joseph Butler, Dissertation "On the Nature of Virtue," appended to *The Analogy of Religion Natural and Revealed*, Morley's Universal Library Edition (London: George Routledge & Sons, 1884), p. 302.

30. Ibid., p. 301.

31. This and the next two paragraphs are drawn from J. B. Schneewind, "Moral Crisis and the History of Ethics," pp. 525-39 in *Midwest Studies in Philosophy*, vol. 8: *Contemporary Perspectives on the History of Philosophy*, ed. Peter A. French, Theodore E. Uehling, Jr., and Howard K. Wettstein (Minneapolis: University of Minnesota Press, 1983).

32. Fried, p. 34.

6. Moral Knowledge: The Limits of Redeemed Freedom

1. Exodus 20:1-2.

2. Galatians 1:4; Ephesians 1:21.

3. Corinthians 1:22; 5:5.

4. Romans 12:2; Galatians 2:20.

5. Augustine, *City of God*, I, 29.

6. Cf. Michael Walzer, *Spheres of Justice* (New York: Basic Books, 1983).

7. H. L. A. Hart, *The Concept of Law* (Oxford: Clarendon Press, 1961), p. 189ff.

8. *Summa Theologiae*, IaIIae, q. 94, a. 2.

9. Ibid., a. 4.

10. E. A. Goerner, "On Thomistic Natural Law: The Bad Man's View of Thomistic Natural Right," *Political Theory* 7 (February 1979): 114ff.

11. Ibid., p. 115.

12. Peter Geach, *The Virtues* (London: Cambridge University Press, 1977), p. 17.

13. Josef Pieper, *The Silence of Saint Thomas* (New York: Pantheon Books, 1957), p. 96.

14. Ephesians 4:13. I do not wish to underestimate the difficulties involved in specifying what it would mean to be "like Christ" or to "follow Jesus." For a very careful delineation of the issues, see Gene Outka, "Following at a Distance: Ethics and the Identity of Jesus," pp. 144-160 in Garrett Green, ed., *Scriptural Authority and Narrative Interpretation* (Philadelphia: Fortress Press, 1987).

15. Luke 2:41ff.

16. Matthew 20:1ff.

17. Reinhold Niebuhr, *The Nature and Destiny of Man*, vol. 2: *Human Destiny* (New York: Charles Scribner's Sons, 1964), p. 69.

18. Dietrich Bonhoeffer, *Ethics* (New York: Macmillan, 1955), pp. 120ff.

19. Ibid., p. 124f.

20. Ibid., p. 139f.

21. Helmut Thielicke, *Theological Ethics*, vol. 1: *Foundations* (Philadelphia: Fortress Press, 1966), p. 257.

22. Ibid.

23. Ibid., p. 263.

24. Psalm 103:3-4.

25. Augustine, *City of God*, XV, 5.

26. *City of God*, V, 17.

27. Ibid.

7. Salvation and Politics, Church and Society

1. See Mark 1:15.

2. Corinthians 6:2.

3. Augustine, *City of God*, XX, 8.

4. See R. A. Markus, *Saeculum: History and Society in the Theology of St. Augustine* (Cambridge: Cambridge University Press, 1970), pp. 20f.

5. Augustine, *City of God*, XI, 1.

6. Cf. Markus, p. 31.

7. Edmund S. Morgan, ed., *Puritan Political Ideas, 1558-1794* (Indianapolis: Bobbs-Merrill, 1965), p. 246.

8. Markus, p. 23.

9. See Acts 1:7; I Thessalonians 5:1-2.

10. Eric Voegelin, *Science, Politics and Gnosticism* (Chicago: Henry Regnery, 1968), p. 93.

11. Paul Tillich, *The Protestant Era* (Chicago: University of Chicago Press, 1957), p. xv.

12. Ibid., p. 46f.

13. Quoted in James Luther Adams, Wilhem Pauck, and Roger Lincoln Shinn, eds., *The Thought of Paul Tillich* (San Francisco: Harper & Row, 1985), pp. 371, 364.

14. Gustavo Gutierrez, *We Drink from Our Own Wells: The Spiritual Journey of a People* (Maryknoll, N.Y.: Orbis Books, 1984), p. 8.

15. Ibid., p. 20.

16. Michael Walzer, *Exodus and Revolution* (New York: Basic Books, 1985), p. 7.

17. Ibid.

18. Ibid., p. 108f.

19. Michael Goldberg, *Jews and Christians: Getting Our Stories Straight* (Nashville: Abingdon Press, 1985).

20. Ibid., p. 154f.

21. Walzer, p. 123.

22. Reinhold Niebuhr, *Moral Man and Immoral Society* (New York: Charles Scribner's Sons, 1932), 70f.

23. Augustine, *City of God*, XIX, 24.

24. See Ralph Lerner, "Commerce and Character: The Anglo-American as New-Model Man," in *Liberation South, Liberation North*, ed. Michael Novak (Washington and London: American Enterprise Institute for Policy Research, 1981), p. 26.

25. Ibid.

26. In Morgan, ed., *Puritan Political Ideas*, pp. 222-23.

27. Jean-Jacques Rousseau, *The Social Contract* (New York: Penguin Books, 1968), IV, 8 (p. 181).

28. Ibid.

29. Ibid., II, 7 (p. 84).

30. Ibid., IV, 8 (p. 186).

31. Augustine, *City of God*, IV, 4.

32. "Justice in the World," in *The Gospel of Peace and Justice: Catholic Social Teaching since Pope John*, presented by Joseph Gremillion (Maryknoll, N.Y.: Orbis Books, 1976), p. 514. For a review and analysis of some of the debate that followed publication of this document, see Charles M. Murphy, "Action for Justice as Constitutive of the Preaching of the Gospel: What did the 1971 Synod Mean?" *Theological Studies* 44 (June 1983): 298-311.

33. "Evangelii Nuntiandi," in *Proclaiming Justice & Peace: Documents From John XXIII-John Paul II*, ed. Michael Walsh and Brian Davies (Mystic, Conn.: Twenty-Third Publications, 1984), p. 217.

34. Ibid., p. 216.

35. Ibid., p. 212.

36. Ibid., p. 210.

37. Francis Schüssler Fiorenza, "The Church's Religious Identity and Its Social and Political Mission," *Theological Studies* 43 (June 1982): 200.

38. Ephesians 4:12.

39. See Matthew 25:31-46.

40. Cited in Paul Johnson, *A History of Christianity* (New York: Atheneum, 1980), p. 75.

41. Ibid.

42. See Galatians 6:10: "As we have opportunity, let us do good to all men, and especially to those who are of the household of faith."

43. Gustaf Aulen, *The Faith of the Christian Church* (Philadelphia: Fortress Press, 1960), p. 377.

44. Ibid.

45. Max L. Stackhouse, *Apologia* (Grand Rapids, Mich.: Eerdmans, 1988), p. 184.

46. Ibid., p. 185.

47. Helmut Thielicke, *Theological Ethics*, vol. 2: *Politics* (Philadelphia: Fortress Press, 1969), p. 550.

8. Morality: The Measure of our Days

1. Stephen Sapp, *Full of Years: Aging and the Elderly in the Bible and Today* (Nashville: Abingdon Press, 1987), p. 33.

2. See Ernest Becker, *The Denial of Death* (New York: The Free Press, 1973).

3. Harold R. Moody, "The Meaning of Life and the Meaning of Old Age," in *What Does It Mean to Grow Old?: Reflections from the Humanities*, ed. Thomas R. Cole and Sally A. Gadow (Durham, N.C.: Duke University Press, 1986), p. 38.

4. E. B. White, *Charlotte's Web* (New York: Harper & Row, 1952). Citations will be identified by page numbers in parentheses within the body of the text.

5. Felix Salten, *Bambi* (New York: Grosset & Dunlap, 1929). Citations will be identified by page numbers in parentheses within the body of the text.

6. Seneca, "On Tranquility of Mind," in *Moral Essays*, vol. 2 (London: William Heinemann, 1951), XI, 1.

7. C. S. Lewis, *The Last Battle* (New York: Macmillan, 1956). Citations will be identified by page numbers in parentheses within the body of the text.

8. Cf. Reinhold Niebuhr, *The Nature and Destiny of Man*, vol. 2: *Human Destiny* (New York: Charles Scribner's Sons, 1964), p. 287: "Everything in human life and history moves toward an end. By reason of man's subjection to nature and finiteness this 'end' is a point where that which exists ceases to be. It is *finis*. By reason of man's rational freedom the 'end' has another meaning. It is the purpose and goal of his life and work. It is *telos*. . . . The problem is that the end as *finis* is a threat to the end as *telos*."

9. Cf. Cicero, "De Senectute," in vol. 20 of the Loeb Classical Library (London: William Heinemann Ltd., 1923), XIX, 69: "[T]o me nothing whatever seems 'lengthy' if it has an end; for when that end arrives, then that which was is gone; naught remains but the fruit of good and virtuous deeds."

10. Becker, p. 26.

11. Psalm 42:1-2.

12. Psalm 84:1-3.

13. Leon R. Kass, *Toward a More Natural Science: Biology and Human Affairs* (New York: The Free Press, 1985), p. 312.

14. Cicero, *De Senectute*, XIX, 66.

15. Helmut Thielicke, *Death and Life* (Philadelphia: Fortress Press, 1970), p. 15.

16. Ibid., p. 110.

17. *De Senectute*, X, 33.

18. Isaiah 65:20. Cf. Sapp, p. 68.

19. Cicero, *De Senectute*, XX, 76.

20. Sapp, p. 149f.

21. Daniel Callahan, *Setting Limits: Medical Goals in an Aging Society* (New York: Simon and Schuster, 1987), p. 66.

22. Kass, p. 306.

23. Ibid., p. 307.

24. Ibid., p. 316.

25. Ibid.

26. Cicero, *De Senectute*, XIX, 71.

27. Lewis Thomas, "The Deacon's Masterpiece," pp. 130-36 in *The Medusa and the Snail* (New York: Viking Press, 1979).

28. Paul Ramsey, *The Patient as Person* (New Haven and London: Yale University Press, 1970).

29. Ibid., p. 144ff.

30. Cf. Niebuhr, p. 321: "From the standpoint of such a faith history is not meaningless because it cannot complete itself; though it cannot be denied that it is tragic because men always seek prematurely to complete it."

31. Norman Daniels, *Am I My Parents' Keeper?: An Essay on Justice Between the Young and the Old* (New York and Oxford: Oxford University Press, 1988), p. 87.

32. Albert Camus, *Reflections on the Guillotine* (Michigan City, Ind.: Fridtjof-Karla Publications, 1959).

33. Ibid., p. 42ff.

34. Cicero, *De Senectute*, XVIII, 65.

35. John Baillie, *A Diary of Private Prayer* (New York: Charles Scribner's Sons, 1949), p. 129.

9. The Taste for the Other

1. Alasdair MacIntyre, *Three Rival Versions of Moral Enquiry: Encyclopaedia, Genealogy, and Tradition* (Notre Dame, Ind.: University of Notre Dame Press, 1990), p. 80.

2. My interest in the contrast between these two paradigmatic "Confessions" was first stimulated and informed by Ann Hartle, *The Modern Self in Rousseau's Confessions: A Reply to St. Augustine* (Notre Dame, Ind.: University of Notre Dame Press, 1983). Hartle suggests that Rousseau did, in fact, intend to provide a contrasting account of human nature, one that would be a "reply" to Augustine's account. When citing Augustine's *Confessions* below, I will use the translation of Rex Warner (New York: New American Library, 1963) and will give book and chapter number within parentheses in the text. When citing Rousseau's *Confessions*, I will use the translation of J. M. Cohen (Harmondsworth:

Penguin Books, 1953) and will give page number within parentheses in the text.

3. Cf. Margaret R. Miles, "Infancy, Parenting, and Nourishment in Augustine's *Confessions*," *Journal of the American Academy of Religion* 50 (1982): 359: "All of Augustine's talk of growth in the Christian life, then, relies on the necessity of returning to the infancy condition. . . ." It is not, of course, an entirely original theme! See Luke 18:16-17.

4. Peter Brown, *Augustine of Hippo* (Berkeley: University of California Press, 1967), p. 50. Cf. Rousseau's account of a petty theft he once perpetrated: "Nothing could have been so far from my natural disposition as this act. But I note it as a proof that there are moments of a kind of delirium, in which men cannot be judged by what they do" (p. 46).

5. This contrast was first called to my attention by Elizabeth Ann Misch.

6. Jean-Jacques Rousseau, *The Reveries of the Solitary Walker* (New York: Harper & Row, 1982), p. 65.

7. Ann Hartle has pointed out to me that (in V, 3) Augustine grants that the natural philosophers had some genuine understanding of our world, though not its Creator. Moreover, in X, 35, he says that knowledge of nature is "not beyond our ken." Hartle has noted that Warner (p. 246) gets this wrong in translating "the workings of nature which is beyond our ken" — precisely the opposite of what Augustine says. Thus, to say that created being is ultimately mysterious does not mean that it is entirely unknowable. In fact, for Augustine both the possibility that it can be known and its ultimate unfathomability are grounded in the Creator who orders the natural world but whose ordering can never be fully grasped by our intellects.

8. Robert J. O'Connell, *St. Augustine's Confessions: The Odyssey of Soul* (Cambridge, Mass.: Harvard University Press, 1919), p. 133.

9. Robert E. Meagher, *Augustine: An Introduction* (New York: Harper & Row, 1979), p. 192ff.

10. Ibid., p. 108.

11. Warner (p. 210) translates: "Let me know you, my known. . . ." This is, however, a mistranslation. In *Sources of the Self: The Making of the Modern Identity* (Cambridge,

Mass.: Harvard University Press, 1989), Charles Taylor has recently argued that modern "inwardness" and emphasis on a free inner self begins with Augustine. He sees Augustine as the one who bequeathed "the inwardness of radical reflexivity" to our tradition of thought. Yet, Taylor also grants that for Augustine the turn inward is always seen as a way to something outside the self; the path inward is the way to God, who is the ultimate Other. And certainly Augustine's inwardness has a very different character from the modern identity as Taylor describes it, since Augustine could not conceive of personal identity as a work of self-creation.

12. Rousseau, *Reveries*, p. 68.

13. Ibid. The italics are Rousseau's.

14. Ibid., p. 68f.

15. John J. O'Meara, *The Young Augustine* (London and New York: Longman, 1980), p. 13.

16. Consider the following: I, 1 begins: "Great art thou, O Lord, and greatly to be praised." When in XI, 1 Augustine turns from his present life to topics cosmological, we see the same passage cited. In I, 1 Augustine writes: "And man wants to praise you, man who is only a small portion of what you have created"—a formulation that seems to invite the later consideration of the Genesis story. The famous description of the restless heart in I, 1 seems to find its answering note in XIII, 35, when Augustine writes: "Lord God, give us peace—for you have granted us all things—the peace of quiet, the peace of the Sabbath which has no evening." Finally, in I, 1 Augustine cites the passage which says "they that seek shall find him." And he concludes the *Confessions* in XIII, 38 with these words: "This must be asked of you, sought in you, knocked for at you. So shall it be received, so shall it be found, so shall it be opened."

17. Augustine, *Ennarrationes in Psalmos*, 86.9. Cited in Meagher, p. 282.

Index

209